D0913132

SON OF A
MILKMAN
MY CRAZY LIFE WITH TESLA

BRIAN WHEAT
WITH CHRIS EPTING

Post Hill
PRESS

A POST HILL PRESS BOOK

Son of a Milkman:
My Crazy Life With Tesla
© 2020 by Brian Wheat
All Rights Reserved

ISBN: 978-1-64293-615-5
ISBN (eBook): 978-1-64293-616-2

Cover art by Cody Corcoran
Interior design and composition, Greg Johnson, Textbook Perfect

Post Hill Press
New York • Nashville
posthillpress.com

Published in the United States of America

1 2 3 4 5 6 7 8 9 10

To my mother, Amelia, the greatest woman I ever knew.

SET LIST

FOREWORD

BY JOE ELLIOTT

It was 1986, and Def Leppard was in Holland working on the album that would become *Hysteria*. Our manager, Peter Mensch, came over to the studio one day with a cassette and said, "I want you to hear this new band we just signed." It was Tesla. I remember standing there with Phil Collen, listening, and we look at each other and agree they sound great! I remember thinking, *Wow, they even remind me a little bit of us!* Then the cassette ends, and it automatically begins playing the B-side. All of a sudden we're hearing a board tape of an Alice Cooper show, and it sounds absolutely incredible. I mean, at that point we knew we would soon be looking for a sound engineer, and what made this Cooper show so incredible was that the vocals just sounded huge. And Kip Winger's voice sounded like twenty people! We knew our new album would be a challenge to replicate live, and whoever that sound engineer was, well, we had a feeling he was our guy! So all of a sudden we go from, "Wow, Tesla's great!" to "Who is the sound engineer?" and "We have to have him!"

Cut to 1987, and Tesla's name came up as an opening act for us when we were getting ready to tour the UK and Ireland. We thought back to that cassette and thought, "Oh yeah, those guys are really good, yes! Great stuff!" Now, in this book you're reading right now, Brian says that I ignored him on that tour. Bastard! For the record, I have no memory of that, but I will say I may have had my head up my ass at that point because we finally had a hit album in our own country. After ten years! That's longer than the Beatles were together! So, yes, maybe I was not paying attention to everybody backstage with all the attention that was on us back then, but honestly, the main reason I hardly ever saw Tesla was because more often than not, when they were on stage playing we would just be arriving to the gig, and by the time we started playing, there were usually gone! It never occurred to me that there was a lack of bonding with Brian and his bandmates. But hey, this is Brian's book, so I'm going to let his version stand as is!

But I do remember distinctly that our connection started right before the first gig on the American tour in October 1987. We were starting in Glens Falls, in upstate New York. We were staying in this chalet kind of ski resort hotel, and after we finished sound checking at the final rehearsal, we went back to the hotel. Tesla sound checked after us, and so they got back later. Brian was staying in the room next to me, and through the walls I could hear him playing all of these songs by The Beatles and Wings. Now, in Def Leppard, I'm the guy who's truly the biggest McCartney fan, and as I learned that night, in Tesla, Brian Wheat is the guy who is absolutely the most McCartney-mad. So I knocked on the door to see if I could hang out, and in his room that night, singing songs from *Ram*, *Red Rose Speedway*, and other classic McCartney albums, we bonded over our love of all things Macca! Like me, he knew everything, from the bootlegs to the studio recordings and everything in between. That's the night our friendship was really born. From that point on, we hung out whenever we could. And without fail, we would bust each other's balls, just having fun and becoming friends. I remember one show in Toronto at a baseball stadium where we would be playing after the baseball game was over. Earlier in the day the stage was wheeled out onto the field where it would be later so we could do a sound check. Out there in that empty stadium I remember first racing model cars with Brian and then, after months of good-natured banter, we finally did a hundred-meter dash because he was convinced he would trounce me...wrong! Yes, it's Wheaty's book, but *this* truth stands!

For Brian and me, it's more than music; it's kinship. I know he thinks of me like his big brother, and that's why we can poke fun at each other, and we do! I never had a little brother, so he's my pretend little brother, and he takes the brunt of everything I never got to do to a real one. Having said that, though, Brian is somebody I have total respect for because he's worked very hard for all he has and has contributed so much to why Tesla is still out there playing shows all these years later. Now, back in the '90s when a lot of us struggled when music changed, he managed to keep both his head and band above water. He never gives up, and I give him lots of credit for that. While we can be very sarcastic with each other, we also trust each other. I have the kind of relationship with him where, if he's down, I can be brutally honest with him, and he doesn't fall out with me because of that. He trusts me because he knows I really care about him. That's why he calls me up in the first place if he needs council. He knows he's not going to get bullshit from me. I'm going to say, "Listen motherfucker, you need to take care of this, you have to have a really good think about what you just said and what it really means." We've had so many conversations over the years where he would say to me, "I know, I know, I know, *but*—!" Then I would step in and say, "There's no *buts* here!" Whether it involves his health issues or band matters, I'm always going to be forthright and honest with him because of how much I care about him. Brian has shared many dramatic incidents that have happened in this life with me because he knows they'll be discussed with a lot of humor, love, and respect. He knows that no matter how brutally honest I might be, it's coming from a good place because, again, I truly care about him. In a way it reminds me of how Def Leppard's producer, Mutt Lange, was with me when I needed advice, and he always tried to help me. You learn from that. You pass that knowledge along when you make a friend that you care about.

Brian has written an open and very honest book that I think you will thoroughly enjoy. I'm proud of how he has dealt with a lot of the things he struggles with, but I'm equally proud of the great music he and his band have made over the years. Love you, man!

Joe Elliott
May 2020

PREFACE

A couple of things about my book. When you write a memoir, they tell you it's important to figure out what your voice is. I think what I've learned in putting this book together is that my voice is all over the map. It's just my personality. I jump around a lot. Part of it is that I have a lot of things going on in my life at all times, but part of it is just my personality. As you will learn in these pages, I have a few issues. I struggle on a daily basis with general anxiety disorder, occasional depression, a bit of OCD, and a host of autoimmune diseases that can make life really tough sometimes. I think I struggle day-to-day in ways that most "rock stars" don't. But hey, that's part of the reason I wrote this book. Maybe some of you out there will find me more relatable. Maybe some of the things that I say will help you cope with whatever disorder or issue that you are experiencing. The bottom line is, this is how I talk. I am what I am, and I wasn't about to try and make it all pretty just because I was writing a book. Just like you are you, this is me. Cool? OK, let's get on with the story.

Prologue

My friend, the legendary photographer Ross Halfin, invited me to come along one day while he was shooting around West Hollywood. Ross has shot everybody, it seems, and he started photographing my band, Tesla, back in the late '80s when we were on one of our first big tours with Def Leppard. When I started getting into photography, he became a mentor to me. He actually got me my first camera. Anyway, if Ross ever invited you to tag along for a photo session, you didn't say no. It was even more special because he was going to be shooting Chris Cornell.

It was a casual thing, just the three of us cruising around Los Angeles, pulling over from time to time so that the iconic Soundgarden front man could get out and strike a few poses along the boulevard. I had never met Chris before, but I was a big fan. His dark, brooding brilliance made him one of the definitive artists of his generation, so I was extra anxious about tagging along. Chris was cool. If fans noticed him on the street while Ross was shooting, he took a minute to say hello and was totally accommodating. Not everybody is like that.

What really struck me about Chris, though, was what we talked about in the car. I can't even remember how the subject came up, but we started talking about anxiety and depression. I had no idea what he was going through in his life, but he spoke candidly about the forces that were bringing him down, tearing at his psyche. *Fuck, Chris Cornell?* I thought. He knew nothing about me, so there's no way he could've been aware that I had been suffering from deep anxiety issues for most of my life. It was a strange thing to bond over in the car, but we did. We related over the issues we both were having, and while I felt sad for what he was going through, there's always something positive about someone who can relate to what you are dealing with. I felt like he was a kindred spirit. Driving around that day watching Ross take pictures and talking with Chris is something that has really stuck with me. Chris Cornell could not help but make a strong impression on you. He was just that powerful of a personality. It was the only time I was ever in his presence.

About three years later, I saw the news that he had taken his life. I was devastated. That was in May 2017. Two months later, Chester Bennington of Linkin Park did the same thing. Soon after that, Anthony Bourdain. Gone. What the fuck? This was getting out of control. To most people, it probably seemed inexplicable. These guys were at the top of their game, right? How could they kill themselves? Well, if you suffer from anxiety and depression, you know appearances have little to do with what's real. There's perception, and then there's the brutal reality of mental illness.

In the summer of 2019, Tesla was on tour throughout Canada playing with our old pals, Def Leppard. Thirty years after touring with them on the *Hysteria* Tour, we were still tight. They were still like our big brothers. I should've been on top of the world. Everything was great...on the outside. Inside, I was dying. My anxiety had given way to what I knew was a deepening depression.

I was sleeping so much more because I didn't want to get out of my bunk on the bus. I didn't even know why. I was just starting to circle a deep and dark vortex. I could feel it sucking me down. And I kept thinking of Chris, Chester, Anthony, and everybody else I knew who was experiencing the paralyzing effects of depression. I felt like I was going down. I felt like this might be the end. Or at least the start of the end. This was the scariest and darkest moment I have ever encountered. I didn't want to wake up. I didn't know how to wake up.

Me & Eleanor

I was born November 5, 1962, at the county hospital in Sacramento, California. I was an illegitimate child, and my father was the milkman. He came around, dropped off a little milk and cream, and then flew the coop. Literally. You've heard the term "son of a milkman," based on the old joke that way back when, when the husband was at work, the wife would fool around with the milkman and end up pregnant? Well, that's me. I have lived that joke since day one.

There's a lot of history in Sacramento. In 1848, when gold was discovered by James W. Marshall at Sutter's Mill in nearby Coloma (about fifty miles away), lots of people were drawn to the area. This city was incorporated in 1850 and today is the oldest incorporated city in California. It became the state capital in 1879. Sacramento became the western end of the Pony Express and then later a terminus of the first transcontinental railroad. A lot of interesting people come from Sacramento, including the actors LeVar Burton, Timothy Busfield, and Sam Elliott. Country singer Lynn Anderson is from Sacramento along with Timothy B. Schmit of the Eagles, as well as a lot of great bands, including Papa Roach and of course, Tesla.

I grew up in South Sac, a lower-middle-class part of town. Sacramento has a whole lot of government workers. It's grown a lot. It was kind of a medium-sized town when I was young, and now I guess you'd say it's a small city. I lived there until 2018.

Even though I'm known as Brian Wheat, Wheat is not my real last name. My mom, Amelia, was married to Buddy Wheat, this crazy guy from Oklahoma. He was an alcoholic who used to beat the shit out of her. She had four kids with him: Buddy Jr., born in 1950, Shari, born in 1951, Mike, born in 1953, and David, born in 1954. She had my other brother, Timmy, with another guy. Timmy is three years older than me.

I was her second illegitimate child. My mom couldn't deal with it and decided that she was going to put me up for adoption. My aunt Annie managed to talk her out of it, but I was on the auction block for about five days, and it bites on me to this day. After Timmy was born, my aunt Toni laid down the law, telling my mom she didn't want her having any more children. When my mom got pregnant with me, she was terrified of what Toni would say. Her way out was to pick a fight with Toni. They wound up not speaking for seven years. Being illegitimate was hard on me. There weren't a lot of kids that were in my situation, which made me very self-conscious. That's where I think this scarring came from, just being different. Kids at school would look at you weirdly or make hurtful comments. Now I look at it as a badge of honor. I never used it as an excuse, and I persevered. I can even joke about it, but it did leave emotional scars.

Back in 1962, society frowned upon women having illegitimate children, so my mom gave me the last name of Wheat. My biological father was this guy by the name of Norm Farrand. He was the milkman and was around after my mom had Timmy. She was really anti-men at the time. He would come for the check for milk, and she would just hand it over and slam the door in his face. Evidently, he finally got her to go out on a date, and they went out for about six months. After he got her pregnant with me he fucked off to Illinois.

I have a half-brother named Gary who is Norm's son. He's almost exactly a year younger than me, but I never talked to him growing up. When I was about twelve years old, my mom told me about Norm and took me to Illinois to see him. I thought my godfather, Cecil, was my dad, but my sister told me the truth when I was a little kid. She said, "He's not your dad. Your dad is Norm, the milkman." When Mom took me to see him around Christmas, we ran into Gary and his stepsister, or half-sister maybe, at the mall. They got in the car with me and my dad, and we gave them a lift to their house. That's how we were introduced to each other.

Years later I would be in Gary's wedding. By then he worked for the city of Chicago and lived outside of Waukegan. He worked for the water department, civil service, drove a snowplow. He was there forever. When Norm died I didn't even go to the funeral. Gary told me about it. I said, "Hey, sorry to hear that." I wasn't very close to Norm. We had kind of a weird relationship. I met him when I was twelve and saw him again when I was fifteen. The last time I saw him was when Tesla was on tour with Def Leppard in 1988. He came to a gig at the Horizon in Chicago.

A few months later he called me drunk and asked for $50,000. I told him to fuck off. I was fucked up, too, so it was kind of amusing. He would call occasionally. He'd be drunk and talk shit, and I'd tell him to go fuck off or I'd come through the phone and whip his old ass. All through my twenties and thirties he'd call me when he was fucked up, all drunk, and would sing or ask me for money. I'd call him every now and again when I was married to my first wife, trying to be a good guy.

The sad thing about it is when I got old enough to not have any grudges toward him, he had dementia, so he didn't know what was going on. I managed to go see him with Gary in 2000 while he was in the hospital. He knew it was me, and he knew it was Gary. That was kind of my making peace with him. I know Gary was stoked. But I didn't attend his funeral. Like I tried to tell Gary, I didn't know him. I didn't have a relationship with him. It was all about my mom. He never paid a dime of child support.

When I was young I had a lot of animosity towards Norm. When I got older and went through all kinds of therapy, I kind of forgave him. Then again, I never knew him, so you can't have any feelings for somebody you don't really know. I don't have any regrets. I don't think, "I wish I knew my father, he was this great guy, I wish we had a relationship." I'm fine with it. He didn't have a big impact on me.

I didn't feel compelled to jump on a plane and go back there. If I had, it would have been for Gary's sake. Gary didn't hold it against me, so I don't regret it, not really. It's the way I felt at the time. If he died again today I would probably go, because it's been ten years since he died. It's like, fuck it, you know, you die, and I didn't know you. Really? What good does it do if I come to your funeral? Some people might have thought I was being a bit cold-blooded, sayin' fuck you, my last fuck you, and maybe it was, I don't know. I think I feel different about it now.

The cool thing is I got a brother out of it. Me and Gary are cool. We don't see each other that much, but every time I'm in Chicago I see him. We talk all the time. We're as close as me and my other brothers, with the exception of my older brother, Buddy. I don't see Mike or David or Timmy that often. The guys that I see all the time are the guys in Tesla, and that's how it's been since I was eighteen. Frank Hannon and Jeff Keith are like brothers to me. I've accumulated way more hours with those two guys than I did with my actual family, the people that are my blood. Nothing against those guys, I'm really close to Buddy, we do a lot of shit together, and we've always been pretty tight. But I'm always busy. They don't understand it, the rest of them. They can't comprehend it. Buddy does. I don't know if the others think that I'm just lying around counting money all the time. Unfortunately, a lot of people think that, and it's not necessarily the truth. I wish it were, but it's not. There's usually money to be counted, but it's mostly just for the bills I've got to pay. They have no concept of that. In all fairness, though, nor do a lot of people. Unless you're living it, you can't explain it.

BACK IN THE '60S, WHAT I REMEMBER is having all these brothers and my sister, and there was always music in the house. The first real memories of music are from 1966 when I was four. I had a Close 'n Play toy record player. "When Johnny Comes Marching Home," "Supercalifragilistic," all that little-kid stuff. I used to grab my brothers' records and put them on. The first real record I played was *Revolver*, the Beatles classic, which is probably why I'm such a huge Beatles fan. The first song I can really remember listening to is "Eleanor Rigby." Paul McCartney's voice was soothing. It's hard to describe what his voice did to me. There was something calming and mysterious about it, and it just made me feel good. That's the voice I wanted to hear all the time: singing songs, reading me stories, whatever. Little did I know the effect that voice would have on my life later on. He became my musical hero early on in life.

I think the other reason I gravitated toward grabbing *Revolver* was the artwork, because the line drawing that Klaus Voormann did looked like a cartoon. I remember "Eleanor Rigby" because when I tried to play the first song on the album, "Taxman," there was a scratch. It wouldn't play, so I had to go to the second song, and that's what started me on my quest. I was also hearing Cream, Jimi Hendrix, Janis Joplin, Moby Grape, and Blue Cheer—all that stuff—coming from my brothers' rooms. I was well into music by the time I was six years old. If "Taxman" hadn't been scratched, George Harrison might have been my idol!

Along with the music there was always the smell of marijuana coming out of the bedrooms, and I was exposed to a lot of sex. Lucky me, right? I'd walk into a bedroom and catch one of my brothers fucking someone. I probably looked through the window a few times. I could not believe what I was seeing. I was like "Wow! I wanna fuck!" There was just something so strange, compelling, and seductive about it. Believe it or not, I was only about seven or eight when I was trying to jack off. I don't think it worked, though. I remember messing around with some girl when I was seven. I think it was in first grade. She was in first grade, anyway. My brother David busted us in the back yard in a little tent I had made on the side of the house. He told Mom at dinner, and I got my ass whipped. Lesson learned.

My brothers were heavy into stealing bicycles, stripping them in the garage, and selling them. There was a lot of crazy shit going on in my house when I was a kid, but for me it was kind of normal. I remember, out of the blue, Mike had a drum set in his room. I used to go in there and hit the tom-toms. I think if you asked Mike today how he got his first set of drums, I don't think he'd say it was from mowing lawns. I think it was from selling stolen bicycle parts.

My oldest brother, Buddy, is twelve years older than me. In '66 the whole Vietnam War protest thing was going on, and he was one of those hippies. He used to shoot dope, take all kinds of other drugs, and grew his hair long. My mom threw him out of the house for being a long-haired hippie. The funny thing about Buddy is that back in the day he was a hard-core left-wing liberal. Today he's very conservative. He went completely to the other side, like a pendulum. I think as he got older and got more in control of his life (as head of the rice growers' union) that he wound up being very conservative.

Shari is one year younger than Buddy. The first time I saw her, she was nineteen. I didn't know I had a sister until then. She was away at reform school, as she was a bit of a problem child and used to run away a lot. Back then you could call up and say your kid was incorrigible, and they'd put them away in the juvenile detention center. There were no kids' rights. If your mom wanted to whip your ass, you got your ass whipped. One day, when I was about six, this girl walks into the house, picks me up, and starts hugging me. That's my first memory of Shari. Until then it was always my brothers.

As I said, it was Shari who told me that Norm was my father, not my godfather, Cecil Cayocca. He was my mother's boyfriend from the time I was two until I was about thirteen and was in our lives until he died in 1993. I was baptized as a baby, and he stood in at the ceremony. When Shari said, "Cecil's not your father. I'm sorry to have to tell you that, but it is the truth," I didn't believe her. I mean, I didn't *want* to believe her.

But, when I was twelve, my mom sat me down and said, "This is what happened, and I want you to speak to Norm on the telephone." It wasn't long after that I went to Illinois to see him. We were staying at his apartment, and he said he was going out for a pack of cigarettes and didn't come back for about five days. That's the kind of character he was.

My mom raised me, and there was plenty of love in the family. My mom was a caring person and tough, too. She had to raise six children on her own, with no man of the house. That's why my family can be kind of crazy. There were the typical issues between us brothers, the usual dysfunctions. David used to pick on me and Timmy, beat us up and threaten us with stupid kid shit. Every once in a while Mike, who was big for his age, would get pissed off at David and give him a good whomping.

Buddy, who was the oldest by several years, was constantly being told by Mom to keep us younger ones in line, which was pretty much a full-time job. He got tired of doing that, so to keep David and Mike in line, he gave them each five dollars a week to stay out of trouble. I think he wound up not giving them much because they wouldn't behave. After a while they hit him up for ten dollars a week, and that was the end of the bribery-turned-extortion game.

My mom was on welfare until I was thirteen years old and then went to work for the State of California. She did that for about ten years and then started to develop health problems and, in the end, wound up on disability. But during my early childhood she didn't work, she just tried to take care of the family. Buddy was a pretty good kid. He didn't give my mom a lot of trouble. Timmy, Mike, and David were always in trouble with all kinds of shit. Three boys, no role model...they would try and run over my mom. She was a short woman, about five feet tall. She would stand on a chair when you came in at three in the morning, and she'd hit you over the head with a frying pan. Not me, I was always really good. Part of the reason I think I was always good was because I saw what my brothers and sister had done to her, and I didn't want to be like that. I was close to my mom.

She was born in Kenosha, Wisconsin, and her parents were full-blooded Italians who came over from Italy in the early 1900s through Ellis Island. She had quite a large family. Her mother had had eight husbands. My mom was born in 1925, and she moved to Sacramento about ten years later with her mother and her little brother. My mom died in 2006, and we sold her house in 2010.

While she was alive, my mom would come over, and we'd sit up talking till the early hours of the morning. She'd tell me stories about working at McClellan Air Force Base during World War II putting together airplanes. She had several mental breakdowns. I know of three. She went away to the hospital when I was seven, and Cecil's sister, Ethel, took care of me. Then I saw her have one when I was thirteen. I had to take care of her that time. Then, three years before she died, she had another one. I think she had some problems before I was born. I've heard strange rumblings from my brothers and sister that they had to go away and live with some family for about three or four months.

All the chaos around the house probably affected me more than I knew, at least until I got into therapy years later. I've always had this habit when I sit of rocking back and forth, like I'm in a rocking chair. I'd always thought it was just nervous energy, maybe a bit of attention-deficit stuff. But Buddy says that I did it when I was a toddler, like two or three years old. I'd rock myself to sleep that way. It seems likely that I was unconsciously building a little safe zone around myself, to tune out all the craziness. It was a coping mechanism. I still do it today. I rock when I drive. When I'm standing I sometimes sway from side to side. I'm still surrounded by craziness, just a different kind. It's amazing the stuff that sticks with us our whole lives. All of the little habits and patterns seem so connected to our past.

My grandmother used to scare the shit out of me. Her name was Maria Fuma. Here we were in America in the '70s where it was all peace, love, and marijuana, and she came from Italy on a boat in 1906. She didn't really speak English, and Italians were not all that welcome then. She worked in a cannery and only spoke broken English. If I was bad when I was a kid, my mom would say, "If you don't behave I'm going to send you to Grandma's."

And I'd say, "No, Mommy, I'll be good, please don't send me to Grandma's" because when you went to her house, she wanted you in bed at 6:30. She was old school. I didn't want any of that.

Today I think I would feel totally differently, you know, the whole heritage and culture thing. It would be way more interesting to me today, understanding my roots. She died when I was ten. By the time I actually got to know her, I wasn't afraid of her. She was dying of cancer. I enjoyed seeing her when I was ten, and that's when I started to understand her, but when I was six I was terrified of her. She never mistreated me, it's just that she didn't let me sit and watch cartoons. She had a black-and-white television she never turned on. The house smelled of Italian herbs and olive oil. My brother Buddy said that when she was younger she was an amazing cook, but by the time I got there, her idea of breakfast was a big pancake with Karo syrup. It was horrible!

Maria Fuma really got around. She had eight husbands. One of them was a Texan farmer named Guy Easton. He would leave the house after a fight, and she'd chase him down the street with a meat cleaver. The people that lived in my neighborhood, where we lived from the time I was ten until my mom died, used to tell stories about my grandmother chasing Guy down the street with a butcher knife, yelling "I cutoffa you balls you sonofabitch." She had a fuckin' temper, all right.

I went back to Italy with my sister, Shari, and my wife, Monique, in 2014 to look for kin. We went to Calabria, where my grandmother was from, and found her relatives in the same little village. I visited her brother's son and his family. They didn't speak English. We showed up on their doorstep 'cause my sister was relentless. She found out where they lived and blew their minds. We said, "Look, we're your relatives." They were cool. He was a doctor, and the family lived in this really nice house, like a villa, but it was straight up and down, more like a townhouse, four huge floors. His two younger sisters each had their own floors. Now all that's left is his youngest sister. The doctor and the middle sister have died since then. They were as old as my aunts. Now I have no more living aunts or uncles on my mom's side. My mom's sister, Aunt Toni, just died, too. She was ninety-nine.

I go to Italy all the time now. Calabria is in the southern part, but I always go north, to Tuscany. That's where I go hang out. It's a little nicer, a little more scenic. But actually, I like the food in the South; it's a little spicier there. I can't drink the water in Italy though. I had a problem the first few times I went over, and then my doctor figured out it was the water, the ice cubes. So when I'm there I gotta drink bottled water or diet coke.

MY MOM PUT ME IN SCHOOL when I was four and a half. Because of where my birthday fell, I had to do first grade twice. I went to Ethel I. Baker Elementary School. When we'd have those father-and-son events, everyone would have their father, and I'd have Buddy. That kind of broke my heart. We always lived in rental houses. We had to move quite a bit because my brothers were getting in trouble all the time, and the neighbors would get our landlord to kick us out. In the fifth grade we moved into my grandmother's house. She had died and left her house to my Aunt Toni because my mom, with five kids and being on welfare a lot of the time, was considered irresponsible. Toni and my other five aunts and uncles made a deal with my mom that we could live there as long as my mom didn't remarry and have any more kids!

I went to Peter Burnett Elementary School after we moved. Then I went to Will C. Wood Junior High School and Hiram Johnson High School. By the time I got to high school there were blacks, Mexican kids, and some Vietnamese kids that were coming over in the late '70s and early '80s. I didn't go to an all-white school, I didn't grow up in an all-white neighborhood, but I didn't grow up in the ghetto either. I wasn't in fear for my life, but I certainly wasn't no silver-spoon kid. You worked in that neighborhood. You didn't fuck around, or you would get your ass kicked.

In school I wasn't very good at English. I'm a bit like Donald Trump. I'm not very well-spoken or well-written either! I was really good in math, and it turned out that that has been useful to me in my career. I was like a C student. Some years I had higher grade averages than others. I liked sports, I played baseball. I got pretty good, too, maybe even college material.

There were a few teachers in my life that I liked. I was really fond of my third grade teacher. I had the hots for her. She's about seventy now. I found her on Facebook. In junior high I had a teacher in a wheelchair. He'd been in a car crash that left him a paraplegic. He could use his arms, but his hands were all fucked up. His name was Mr. Jeffers, and he taught history. I was his assistant in ninth grade. He was cool, and I bonded with him. In high school I had an English teacher, Mr. Lannon, who was just a cool dude. He was another teacher I bonded with, but that was it really.

I had the same friends all through school, these two dudes, Chris Johns and Mike Verras. They were my only two buddies in school. I had one other friend who was my boss at McDonald's, Terry Muñoz. Those were the three friends I had. I didn't meet Terry until I was fifteen. We remained friends through the early Tesla years, when I was trying to make it. From the time I met Frank Hannon, when I was eighteen, me and Terry were together a lot.

I tried to take guitar lessons, but it was too difficult, so I got out of it. From the time I was in eleventh grade I had the McDonald's job. I took three classes in the morning, and the rest of the day I'd go to work. My senior year I cut two of those classes. I made them up at night school so I could graduate on time, which I did.

I had wanted to play music since I was twelve. I really got started because I broke my leg. How that happened was my mom had suffered a nervous breakdown. She was always searching for something, some kind of tranquility. Her doctor was this guy who looked more like a preacher. Oscar Newman was a Seventh-Day Adventist and a cool dude. He'd say, "You know, Amelia, you should try church. It works for me." All of a sudden, I'm twelve years old, and she wants to start attending Seventh-Day Adventist Church. They go on Saturday. I wasn't diggin' that at all. It was fuckin' weird. Other than that, they were pretty much normal; they always had these big cookouts with good food. They did practice vegetarianism and preached being a veggie, which was different for a kid at that time. They had a church outing where they were all going up to the snow in Soda Springs. My mom didn't want me to go and was all pissed off.

I yelled at her, "You never let me do anything!" She let me go. We got up to the snow, and they pulled out these sleds and toboggans. I jumped on a toboggan, crashed into a big tree stump, and broke my leg.

It was my lower leg, the tibia and fibula. They both snapped and were twisted so that my foot was turned around backward. It was fucked up. I don't know if I blacked out when I hit the stump, but when I tried to stand up, my leg was like an accordion. Then I started screaming. I was in shock. It looked like the end of my baseball career before it had even started. They said I'd never run again. But by the time I was thirteen, I was the best player in the league, and I was the fastest motherfucker in the league too!

We were on welfare, so I didn't exactly get the best care. They set my leg wrong. Then they had to break it again. That hurt more than anything. They just cut the calf and put some wedges in, no anesthesia, nothing. My leg's still got a big old knot on it. At the end of the day I was all right. Like I said, by the time I was thirteen, I was playing baseball again after missing the entire previous season. When I was fifteen I was one of the best players in the league. Then I was going to start playing baseball in high school, but at that point I said fuck it, I want to play bass guitar. I don't want to play baseball anymore. That's it, I'm going to be a musician. Buddy wasn't happy about that. Everyone else thought I was nuts. I probably was! All I know is that I had a lot of drive.

Looking back on the way things kind of progressed in my early life, I don't think they were merely a series of disconnected events. Seeing the way my brothers and Shari were, and feeling bad for my mom, set me on a more responsible path. Breaking my leg and changing my focus from sports to music set up the rest of my life. I don't think it is a coincidence that my brother-in-arms, Frank Hannon, also came from a fatherless home, and he also broke his leg, was laid up in bed for months, and that's how he got into music.

Having to constantly battle health issues is my burden to bear. I think everyone has that weight to carry. How you handle it determines whether your path will lead to your goals. Of course you can never see that kind of stuff when you are actually going through it. Only now, entering the backside of my life, can I see the full arc. I think there is a plan for everyone, but not everyone follows it. I think I did, even though I didn't always know that I was. And I certainly strayed from time to time.

In 1975, when I was thirteen, I got colitis for about a year. It's horrible. You shit blood and suffer really bad cramps. This was the first attack I had that was caused by my underlying autoimmune disease. But at the time, they didn't know that. They just gave me some antibiotics to get me going, thinking it was appendicitis or the flu. It took about four months for them to diagnose it, and I probably went to the emergency room a dozen times until they figured it out. My doctor shot me up with antibiotics and put me on a bland diet to settle it down, and I lost a bunch of weight. I had a mild to moderate case, and it went into remission until 1999. Stress is a major trigger of the autoimmune flare-ups, and I sure had a lot of that waiting for me in the years to follow.

The stress also caused anxiety, which would get pretty serious. All of us in the house were stressed, and we had lifelong issues from that. David, Mike, and Timmy are all bipolar. Even Buddy has got some issues because there was so much put on him as a teenager. The first couple of times I smoked pot when I was a teenager, I had pretty serious panic attacks. I didn't smoke pot for a long time after that. It turns out the anxiety was from all these underlying stress issues, and the pot just brought it out.

David and Mike both moved out during this time, and Timmy went to live with his father, so it was just me and my mom until I moved out when I turned eighteen. Timmy moving out was a big blow to my mom. Her goal in life was to keep her family together, in the old world tradition. But it just didn't work out that way. There was too much animosity and disrespect.

Later on, when I was seeing some money from Tesla, the family started hitting me up for cash. Not my mom or Buddy, but the rest of them. And quite frankly, I never gave them very much, no matter what they said it was for. My mom, she got whatever she wanted. And I always helped out Buddy whenever he needed it, even though he never asked. That was the only thing that my mom got upset with me for. She didn't understand why I wouldn't give them money. But I just couldn't do it. Not after what they put her through. And to be truthful, I did give them money. Thousands. Each. But they always wanted more. So I turned off the money spigot. I didn't owe them shit. For my mom it was that Italian family thing. The broken leg put me in a cast from my hip to the bottom of my foot. I think my mom felt bad that I broke my leg, so she bought me an acoustic guitar. Cecil lived on a ranch, and everybody there played guitar. He taught me a country song, "Mosquito on Mah Peetah":

There's a mosquitah on mah peetah, ho ho ho
There's a mosquitah on mah peetah, ho ho ho
There's a dozen on mah cuzzin, you can hear those bastards buzzin'
There's a mosquitah on mah peetah, ho ho ho

Those were the lyrics of the first song I ever learned on guitar, and the chords were a G and a C. I fucked around with that for a while, but I wanted to play the bass because of Paul McCartney. The guitar was too hard. Since then I've learned to play guitar basically to write songs. You don't really write songs on a bass guitar, you write them either on a piano or guitar.

Tuning a guitar was a little frustrating, as there were six strings. McCartney was a bass player, so I wanted to be like Paul McCartney. That was it from day one, from the moment I heard "Eleanor Rigby." I just remember those voices, that stacked harmony, and Paul's voice mainly. From that time on, I was, "Oh, that's that guy, Paul McCartney." I was a McCartney fanatic, whether with the Beatles, Wings, or solo.

The first record I bought with my own money was *Let it Be* when I was eight. Up until that point I didn't have any records. Paul was cool, with the beard, and the four faces of the Beatles on the cover. I didn't know they had broken up. I knew whenever you turned on the radio you heard that voice.

I was lucky to be born in the '60s. There was a real rich period of music between '67 and '75, probably the best period ever, in my opinion. After hearing *Revolver*, I discovered early Beatles stuff in my brothers' record collections: "I Want to Hold Your Hand," "Help," "Can't Buy Me Love," all those early records. I didn't really discover the later Beatles records like *Sgt. Pepper* and *Magical Mystery Tour*. When those Red and Blue greatest hits albums came out, I got the Blue album, their later songs. I thought, *Oh wow, this is all different than those early songs*. I had no idea there were later ones.

In those days I listened to the local station KROY, and KFRC, from San Francisco, on the AM dial. They both played top-forty hits. Then, when I got to be thirteen and fourteen, I started listening to Dave Whitaker on KSFM, and I started hearing bands like Aerosmith, UFO, Montrose, and all that stuff. That's what I used to listen to as a teenager. As I started playing, I started listening to KZAP. DJ Bill Prescott on KZAP would end up being the first to ever play a Tesla song. I took the twelve-inch "Modern Day Cowboy" single to the station, and he played it. Right then and there we were buddies.

In the early '60s, the Rolling Stones played at the Sacramento Memorial Auditorium, and Keith Richards got electrocuted and almost died. The Beach Boys played there as well, and later, Tower of Power. Back then it was the only real place for signed bands to play in Sacramento. My brother Mike took me to see my first show there in 1974. It was the Tubes. "White Punks on Dope" was their hit at the time. They were very theatrical. They had these girls singing background and dancing, and sometimes they were topless, just boobs bouncing around with little pasties on their nipples. That kind of made me want to be a rock star. I remember seeing UFO, Pat Travers, Randy Hansen, Head East, Scorpions, Judas Priest, and Rush, all at the Memorial Auditorium.

I loved UFO. I saw them every time they came to town. They were badass. I was just intrigued by Pete Way, the bass player. He played Gibson Thunderbirds and jumped around. He looked fuckin' cool. That's why I played Thunderbirds and still do. Pete Way was a big influence. He probably wasn't that great of a player, but he sure looked cool, and that's why I liked him.

I was way into English rock bands. I guess the first American thing I really heard and gravitated to was Van Halen in '78. I never really got into the Aerosmith thing when I was a kid. I did much later and grew to appreciate them. Then there was *Ted Nugent*, the first Ted Nugent album. On the tune "Stranglehold" I think there are three notes for the bass in that song. I know five notes now, and I can play the fuck out of them!

When I was fourteen, I started cutting lawns. First it was the woman who lived across the street, then her husband's mother's lawn, then her son's lawn. I used their lawnmowers so I didn't have to pay for gas or fix it when it broke. I had a Schwinn ten-speed bicycle that I bought with the money I earned. When a friend of my brother's was selling his bass guitar for forty dollars, I gave my brother the bike, and he gave me the forty dollars to buy the Mosrite. It was probably the best investment I ever made. Look it up. You can see the Mosrite on the internet. It's kind of like a Fender with a funky neck. The guy in the Ventures played one. I remember it was a red starburst. I sanded it all down to the wood grain so it would look like Paul McCartney's Rickenbacker.

The first amp I had I got at a place called Rader's Music. It was like a PA column, a couple of speakers with volume and one tone control. Then I had a tiny Fender Champ amplifier, and I just started learning to play whatever I was hearing on records or the radio. The first thing I probably learned was Cream's "Sunshine of Your Love." I remember that riff coming out of my brother's bedroom along with the smell of pot. That was the heaviest sound I'd ever heard.

I briefly played a stand-up bass when I was in elementary school when I was eight, but didn't end up pursuing that. I think I wanted to try that because of Paul McCartney, but the thing was bigger than me. The teacher was an old alcoholic and didn't really give a shit. I got bored and quit trying. Schools used to have really good music programs. They don't anymore, and I feel sorry for the kids today.

I didn't get into Led Zeppelin until I was fifteen. I knew this guy, Gary Burns, who played guitar. He turned me on to Black Sabbath, Led Zeppelin, AC/DC, Ted Nugent, and Queen. But up until that point I was all about Wings. Beatles and Wings, that was it for me. I didn't really discover heavier music until '74, '75. That's when I started playing. I started learning that kind of stuff on the bass. We knew another kid, Richard Harvey, who played drums. The three of us would jam in Gary's garage and try to play "Train Kept A-Rollin'." We messed around in that garage for about a year.

That fizzled out, and I started hanging out with this guy named Joe Marietta, who was a really good guitar player. I was fifteen, and he was twenty. He taught me how to play specifics, showing me the bass lines of songs. He went, "This is how it goes, *boom, boom, boom, boom, boom…*" I was just playing by numbers, thinking, *Oh, this goes here.* I had no idea why until then.

When I saw McCartney on TV, he played with a pick. You never saw him play with his fingers. That's why I play with a pick. I'm not very good at playing with my fingers. I actually suck at it. But I can pick the fuck out of it!

I started going out with girls when I was fifteen. I thought it was cool to have a girlfriend, so I began going steady right away. First there was Melinda, then Linda. That's when I started getting into sex. I had gotten my job as the breakfast shift manager at the neighborhood McDonald's, and Linda worked there too. She was a year older than me, and we'd park her car way down at the end of the block and fool around. After a while we'd get a cheap motel room and fuck our brains out. We'd tell our moms that we were spending the night at friends' houses. Linda's mom found my phone number in her room and called it. She and my mom figured out what was going on pretty quick, and we both got grounded for a while. But after that, we were right back at it.

That's when my mom gave me "the talk" about getting someone pregnant and all that. It was good she did that because it did make an impression, and I never got anyone pregnant—that I wasn't married to, anyway!

At sixteen, I started a band called Rage. It was me, Larry Test on vocals, Stacey Nick on drums, and Wendell Polk on guitar. I'd go around to Wendell's house, and we'd sit around and jam. We played backyard keg parties. Kids' parents would go away for the weekend, and we'd throw a party. We'd set up on the patio. There'd be a couple kegs of beer, and we'd jam. That's how you built your following. Wendell is still around. I haven't heard from him in years. I'd love to hear from him. I don't know whatever happened to him. I looked him up on Facebook, but I don't ever hear from him. I'd jam with him. He kind of got me into Black Sabbath and stuff like that. He was into that.

Frank Hannon lived in the same neighborhood I did, but we didn't go to school together, as I had graduated by the time he was a freshman. There were a lot of musicians in South Sac, and Frank used to hang out with some who knew me. He was in a three-piece band that played high schools and keg parties. One night his singer got into a fight with my brother Timmy at a show. Timmy had loaned the band his microphone and wanted to play harmonica with the band, but the singer was being difficult and said no. So, Timmy laid into him and the next thing you know, the cops came, and the show got canceled. People were saying, "Man, that's Brian Wheat's brother." That's how Frank first heard about me.

Back then we rehearsed in the back of an ice factory. The guy who owned it said to us, "My girlfriend's son is fourteen and plays guitar. He'd like to come and jam with you."

We were like, "Yeah, yeah, whatever." One day soon after, this '47 Chevy Classic, a gangster-looking car, rolls up, and this skinny kid gets out of the passenger seat with his Fender Stratocaster and a Marshall amp. If you had a Marshall amp in those years, you were a bad motherfucker. And he was badass. He was better than the guys I was playing with. Suddenly, Wendell's out, and Frank Hannon was in. Then, after a couple of more parties, Joe was out. He didn't want Frank in the band. I think he felt threatened by him. So, now it's me, Frank, Stacey, and Larry. Then Larry was out, and we got Jeff Harper in as singer. That all fizzled out, and Frank and I thought, *Fuck you guys!* and formed Earthshaker.

Just Kidds in the City

Earthshaker came together in 1980 with Jeff Harper (vocals), Bobby Contreras (drums), Paul Contreras (no relation, guitar), Frank, and myself. We got the name from an album by Y&T. Ironically, Y&T were originally named Yesterday & Today, which was the name of a Beatles album! Frank and I built a rehearsal room in the garage at his grandfather's. We were playing AC/DC, UFO, Scorpions, Van Halen, and Def Leppard; that's how we learned to write songs. This guy who lived across the street from me, Rick Jackson, came on the scene and got us into clubs. He took a tape of one of our rehearsals to Steve Clausman, who was booking a club called Gopher's Gulch. It was originally a country music place. They had a mechanical bull and everything. They were featuring rock on some nights, but eventually switched over and renamed the club the Rock Factory. Steve liked the tape and booked us to open for a band he managed called Ian Shelter for twenty-five bucks a night. We kicked their ass!

The local music scene was pretty hot then. You could play in a band and make a living. There were nine or ten clubs in Sacramento, and you could play that circuit. There was the Oasis Ballroom, which was to play a big role in my future. Then there was the Rock Factory, the El Dorado Saloon, C Street North, Shire Road Pub, Galactica 2000, Slick Willy's, The Cattle Club, Club Can't Tell, and Bittercreek Saloon. Today the scene is not so healthy, but several bands have come out of there. Obviously we were the biggest, but there's also the Deftones, Cake, and Papa Roach.

Earthshaker kind of fizzled out, but Frank and I stayed together and started a band called City Kidd with Jeff, Brook Bright on guitar, and Bobby. I think Frank came up with the name. We wanted to change names because musically we were going in a different direction. We wanted to play clubs, so our covers became more commercial. Plus, we started writing originals. That's when that fuckin' new wave shit came out, Flock of Seagulls and Men at Work, so we started playing that shit. Frank and I just wanted to play clubs. Once we had a solid set that was entertaining people, Steve Clausman approached us again. He said, "If you can play this kind of shit, you can play in the clubs and play five nights a week at the Rock Factory."

At the beginning, City Kidd's original material was really bad pop songs with titles like "Teenage Dream," "She's My Only Love," "Tell Me No Lies," and "Be with You"—shit like that. Jeff Harper quit to join a band called Target, and these two girls from Georgetown, a foothill town fifty miles from Sacramento, said, "We know this local singer and he's really good." His name was Jeff Keith. Apparently, he had won a karaoke contest where he wore a pair of headphones and a Walkman and sang along to Sammy Hagar. He came down from the hills one night in 1984, wearing furry white boots. He had this Afro and had never been on stage with a real band. He was holding the microphone about four feet from his mouth. You could barely hear him, and there's all this squealing from the monitors because the sound guy kept trying to turn up his microphone. I thought he sucked, but Frank was next to him and could hear his singing.

He said, "This guy's got a great voice," so we hired him.

Now it's me, Frank, Jeff Keith, Brook, and Bobby. Jeff and Brook didn't get along. Brook was a hard-headed guy, and when he drank, he was obnoxious. They got into a couple of fights. We were doing a showcase in San Francisco one time, and Clausman had booked one room with two beds for the band. Brook brought his girlfriend to the show and decided that they should have one of the beds. I told him, no way, the beds were for the band. Jeff, being the trooper that he is, had already sacked out on the floor in a sleeping bag. When he heard Brook claiming the whole bed, he jumped up and got in his face. Brook told Jeff to fuck off. Well, you say that to Jeff, and you'd best be ready to have a go. So the punches started flying. After they got tired of throwing haymakers, they cooled off and apologized. Brook said, "Yeah we're cool, but if you ever come at me again I'll knock you out." Jeff went charging at Brook. Round two was on! So we got rid of Brook.

We knew about Tommy Skeoch. He played in a band around town called Nasty Habits, who were like the Rolling Stones. Tommy was older, and he looked like a rock star. Frank was very young; he was only fifteen at the time. He looked up to Tommy. Frank was innocent. I don't think Frank had an ego then. He was just a kid who wanted to play music. Tommy looked so cool that Frank and I were always on him to come play with us.

Tommy didn't want to leave Nasty Habits. I remember Frank and I went to his house one time to jam. I had bought this '65 Chevy Bel Air four-door from this woman, Lilly Feather, who went to the same church that my mom went to. We drove that over to Tommy's house in Fair Oaks, which is one of the more affluent Sacramento suburbs. We went up to this little room on the second floor and we jammed. Frank couldn't keep his guitar in tune, and Tommy didn't like that. He said, "Hey man, you should come back and jam again, but Frank should keep his guitar in tune."

A little while later, Tommy came over to Frank's house and we jammed again. That day was great. Bobby was playing drums, and Frank and I were just jamming music, no singer. It sounded great, but Skeoch still didn't want to join us. He was in J. L. Richards at the time, another one of the bar bands playing the circuit. He was making money playing the clubs and we weren't. I remember he brought out a big bag of weed, rolled up this big joint, and smoked it. Skeoch was rockin' out, banging his head, and swinging his long hair all around.

Finally, he joined us. When Skeoch got in the band, all of a sudden we were more of a hard rock band. He just had the whole rock-god thing down pat.

I'm not that precious about my bass playing. I know that I have a style, but I'm not precious about it. I'm more precious about a song I wrote. "Paradise" was a good one. I think I'm good at producing. If you asked me, "What are you?" I'd say, "I'm a producer." Whether it's producing a band, producing a house, creating an environment, you name it. Management and production are my strengths. Songwriting I developed into. I still work on it, but I think I got a couple good ones in there—and a lot of shitty ones!

While we were pulling in big crowds at the clubs, Steve Clausman became our manager. I don't remember signing a management deal, but there certainly was a legal thing, and we wound up paying him back for a lot of the expenses that he had. He was the guy that instilled in us that we had to write our own songs. We went to what we called Clausie Boot Camp. He would make us rehearse five days a week, eight hours a day. He was like a drill sergeant. We hated him. Looking back, though, we completely owe our work ethic to him.

Steve had this checklist of things that we needed to do. Brian, his youngest son, is like my brother. He's my business partner, and like father, like son, they do research, research, research. If they read an article in the *Wall Street Journal* that says you have to follow these five steps to be successful, then they follow those steps. Someone along the line told Clausie, "Send them to vocal lessons, get them groomed, like Brian Epstein." To Steve and Frank's credit, they recognized Jeff's natural ability right away. I didn't like his voice. Shit, was I wrong about that!

Steve got involved with a music lawyer from San Francisco, Bob Gordon. Bob had worked with several Bay Area artists, including Santana, Jefferson Airplane, Janis Joplin, the Doobie Brothers, Van Morrison, and Ronnie Montrose. He hooked Ronnie up with Steve to produce some demos, and we got some pretty decent attention from them. Working with Montrose was a big deal to us, especially where we were from in Northern California. Steve said, "Ronnie Montrose is going to produce some demos for you." We were blown away about that.

Ronnie came in, and we worked on four songs. We had "Tell Me No Lies," "Be With You," "Modern Age Rock," and "Born to Rock." Those last two were Thunderwing songs that we were covering. Thunderwing was a band that my brother Mike played drums in. Ronnie stitched them together and made one song out of it. Ronnie was responsible for a lot that people don't know. The first thing he said to us was, "You got two different styles." We had this Loverboy side like "Teenage Dream," then we had our rock side like "Tell Me No Lies." He said, "You gotta pick a side. You've either gotta be like Loverboy or Def Leppard." *Pyromania* was out at the time, and "Photograph" was huge, so we said we wanted to be like Def Leppard.

He had a song by this European band called Ph.D. It was a keyboard kind of song. Tony Hymas and Simon Phillips were in that band. They both went on to play for Jeff Beck, among others. Ronnie said, "I think this song will be great for you guys, you should do a version of it." It was called "Little Suzi's on the Up" but we just called it "Little Suzi." It sounds completely different than the version we do now. Max Norman produced the version of "Little Suzi" that we play today. He came up with that treatment. But Ronnie brought the song to us. It sounds really light now but was kind of like our version of Loverboy, I suppose, at the time.

In the beginning I think he was amazed at Frank's playing and, obviously, Jeff's voice. I didn't like the recording because Ronnie took the tone knob on my bass and turned it completely off, so there was no definition to the bass, just low-end rumble. Ronnie kind of blew me off. I didn't like him much when we were doing that session. You couldn't talk to him about anything. He was Ronnie Montrose and you weren't. That's OK. He was a brilliant guy, but tortured. Obviously he had demons; he killed himself. Toward the end of his life, he and I became really friendly after I saw him at a Def Leppard concert, around 2001. He was backstage. He was bald, he had cancer...he was just a different guy. He gave me a big hug. So I started speaking with him, and we'd talk on the phone. He told me that when we got signed he told Steve, "Those guys owe me a big flat-screen TV for taking them 'Little Suzi.'"

Years later I called Frank and said, "Let's buy Ronnie a flat-screen TV, because he's told a few people we owe him one." I went to a show he was playing in Modesto. I drove ninety miles with a sixty-five-inch flat screen TV in the back of my SUV.

He doesn't know I'm coming or nothing, and I just roll up to the backstage with it, and he looks at me and says, "Wheat, what the fuck are you doing here?"

I said, "Ronnie, come here." I open the back of the SUV, and out comes this plasma TV. I said, "I know it's late, but here you go." He started crying. Literally in tears. I'd never seen that side of him. When he found out I was good friends with Jimmy Page, he'd ask me for information, like what's he like, and I thought, *Ah, this is cool, man*. I remember when I was a kid with Ronnie. It kind of came around full circle. I enjoyed the last couple of years that we were friends. RIP, Ronnie.

We recorded those songs with Ronnie in Sacramento at the only real pro place there was back then, Heavenly Recording Studios. I was blown away by the whole thing. I didn't really get to hang out in the control room, as that's where all the professionals were. It was really that kind of class thing. The manager and producer were in the control room; you were out in the recording room. It was kind of a trip.

Ronnie was the first one to comment negatively on Bobby's drumming, and Duane Hitchings said the same thing after he got into the producing picture. I think Bobby was blaming me for some of that. But part of that fucked me as well. It was kind of a chicken-and-egg thing. Who's fucking up, the drummer or the bass player? When Troy got in the band, he was really solid, and the next demo sounded like I got incredibly better, but I think Troy gave me something solid to lock on to. I wasn't very good either, and certainly being a bass player you gotta be tight with the drum groove.

Ronnie did some wild shit, changed some sounds around, melodies, lyrics. He definitely produced it, for good or bad. I don't think he was much of an engineer, to be quite honest. Tear the erector set down and rebuild it. That's kind of what he did.

I had moved out of the house with my mom right after I graduated from high school. I moved into a friend's on the same street, but that didn't last long. Eventually I moved in with my girlfriend, Jolene, in her mom's house. At first that was OK, but the more I started playing with the band and enjoying the night life and all that went with it, the more she started getting jealous and resentful. Then we took off for three months to Guam. An agency was sending other bands to do three-month stints there. We went there because Tommy Skeoch had just joined, and we wanted to get tight with him, earn a bunch of money, and have the experience of being away from home, and see if we could live together.

We played at a club called the Pescador, and the clientele was mostly US military because they have air bases on the island. Guam was a small island, about eighteen miles long. I went crazy. I wasn't the type of guy who was into going to the beach. I wasn't getting any pussy. Jeff met his first wife there, so that was good for him. I didn't enjoy it much; I couldn't wait to get off that fucking rock. I learned a lot from it, but it was like doing a jail sentence. Frank, Jeff, and I wrote "Cumin' Atcha Live" while we were in Guam.

We were playing six sets a night, six nights a week. Sunday was our day off, but sometimes people would offer us a lot of money to play somewhere, at the opening of a store or something. So we wound up playing a lot. At the club we did sets of mostly covers and as many originals as we could sneak in. We got tight, but people kept saying that the drummer was weak and we needed to replace him.

This was the first time we had lived with each other. We had two apartments. Tommy, Jeff, and I lived in one apartment, and Frank and Bobby lived in another. We actually behaved pretty well. We were up till four or five in the morning every night, but we never got thrown out or hassled. Maybe we were cool because we were afraid of what Clausie would do to us if we got thrown out. Guamanians were very friendly people. They would have these fiestas which basically were barbecues. If you drove down the street and saw one, you stopped; you had to eat and be sociable.

We had this friend in Guam who was in the navy. I'll call him Ted, to keep him from getting court-martialed. He was cool. He used to steal food from the submarine that he was on and bring us steaks and lobsters and shit. He was on kitchen duty on the sub, and he'd come over and cook these massive meals for us. We also met this guy, Keith. He wasn't navy, just a Guamanian native, a Chamorro, and he'd cook fried chicken and stuff for us.

When we got back from Guam, things between Jolene and me went downhill pretty quickly. We had moved into a house with Jeff and his first wife, Elaine. Jolene was very possessive and jealous. I was just starting to experience the rock-and-roll life, and she wasn't digging it. We began to fight all the time until I just said fuck it. I was going to move back in with my mom, but she laid down all these rules, including a curfew. You're not going to do this; you're not going to do that. I just looked at her and said, "You know what I'm not gonna do? I'm not gonna move back here."

I called Buddy and told him what was going on. I asked him if I could rent a bedroom from him. I moved in with Buddy and stayed there until I bought my first house many years later. Even though I had that argument with my mom, we stayed close. I called her almost every day to make sure she was doing OK. David had gotten out of prison and moved back in there, and then my nephew Butch was living there too. Butch was Shari's son. She had him when she was seventeen. Butch bounced around foster homes when he was a kid. He's five years younger than me, so he's really the younger brother that I never had. He's had a tough life too. His eighteen-year-old son died in a car accident a few years ago.

During Earthshaker, and for a while in City Kidd, I was working at McDonald's, and I could eat all the free food I wanted to, so I did. It was like that documentary, *Super Size Me*. I put on a bunch of weight working there. So I became the fat kid in the band. Then I broke up with Jolene, and now I wasn't getting laid. Who wants to fuck the fat kid?

A subtler effect of being overweight is that it saps your energy and gives you a shitty attitude. I was into the Pete Way vibe on stage, but as I put on the weight, it looked kind of stupid to try and bust moves, and it was tiring. If you're gonna be a rocker, you have to have good aerobics and stamina. So I started to become the stands-in-back-by-the-drums guy. It just creeps up on you, pound by pound, and you don't notice the slide, until one day you're short of breath, your clothes don't fit, and you feel like shit.

There were a lot of jokes and snide remarks about my weight going around the band and audiences. That brought out the obnoxious side of my personality. It came from my insecurity, and I handled the shit by throwing it right back. Whether you deserved it or not sometimes didn't matter. Because the girls didn't want me, I was particularly mean to them. I'd cut them up for any little thing I could think of, their clothes, hair, voice, whatever. I could be a real prick. That was my defense mechanism. It didn't help that I had a sharp tongue and I'm quick-witted. I could shred you up pretty good if you got me going.

It came out in my relationship with the band too. In Guam I would try and assert myself as the guy in charge. Clausman wanted me to do that because he knew I had the personality for it. He wrote me a letter saying how I was the sensible one in the band, and it was up to me to keep everyone out of trouble. He saw that I had leadership capabilities, although I was too young and dumb to see that. I was supposed to keep guys from drinking too much, or partying, or smoking pot. He wanted the club owner to be happy, so I had to keep the sets running on schedule. I'd snap my fingers at the band to get them onstage if we were late, or even if we weren't. I was irritable for any or no reason. Jeff came to me afterwards to try and get me to mellow out. The band actually had a meeting to talk about kicking me out. It was kind of an intervention, and it scared me. It was my dream to play music for a living, not get kicked out of my own band, so I just backed off the authority trip.

My weight was an issue with the band. It was talked about when I wasn't around. Tommy, and later Troy, would say that the band should get a bass player with a better image. I don't think Jeff thought like that. He never has gone for any image shit. Frank always stood by me. He knew I played an important role in the band and felt that I just needed to chill out.

While we were in Guam, Steve Clausman took the tapes from the session with Ronnie and went shopping. He never stopped hustling until we got signed to Geffen. When we came back from Guam, we did showcases in LA at Madame Wong's, the Troubadour, the Country Club, and lots of other places. It was at one of those shows where Duane Hitchings came to see us. He was a songwriter/producer, and he got in with us and completely took us the other way from Ronnie's approach. He had a Grammy, played with Cactus, worked with Kim Carnes, and had co-written "Da Ya Think I'm Sexy" with Rod Stewart.

We were going left, and all of a sudden we made a turn right, but it was good because he taught us how to write songs in more of a commercial arrangement, with melodies too. Real strong, catchy vocal melodies. Basically saying, "Look, you got three minutes on the radio and you can only do so much with that." Now there was a whole second set of demos, with two of the songs kind of rock and two of them kind of pop-rock. While we were doing those demos with Hitchings, Tom Zutaut from Geffen got involved. Zutaut said, "You gotta stay rockin'," and *boom*, Duane was out!

Before he went away, Duane had told us, "Your drummer's got to go, he's holding you back."

We told Bobby, "Hit the drums harder!" He did, and he'd get blisters. The poor guy was missing one and a half fingers that he'd lost in a table-saw accident. It was inevitable. I think, down in his heart, he knew it wasn't working.

Duane knew Herbie Herbert, who managed Journey and the Eric Martin Band. Troy Luccketta played drums with the Eric Martin Band, and they had just broken up, so Duane got Troy to come up to Sac and play with us at the Oasis Ballroom in April of 1984. I used to go see the Eric Martin Band, so I'd seen Troy play. Also, Troy's wife was a friend of my sister's. In one of those thousand-to-one coincidences, my sister lived in the Bay Area, and Troy's wife, Linda, was a stylist who cut her hair. When Troy started playing with us, it was definitely like "Whoa!" Everything went up ten notches.

I remember Troy coming up to Sacramento that day. We were doing a weekend gig or something with Bobby. Everything was hush-hush. Troy came in and set up, and we ran through three or four songs with him. It was pretty obvious that he was what a drummer should sound like in this band: really powerful. So Steve told Bobby he was out and Troy joined. Bobby was bummed out, no two ways about it, but we had to move on. Thankfully, we are still friends with Bobby.

We started playing at the Oasis two nights a month and increased our draw. We were getting six hundred people. When Jeff and I needed extra cash, the owner of the Oasis, Dave Dittman, let us do work stocking the bar. Dave was a great supporter of the band. We were starting to transition from just being a bar band at this time. We had gone from doing four or five nights a week to doing two nights at the Oasis, ninety-minute sets. It was pretty much all originals with maybe a couple of covers. Plus, we were opening for a lot of the national acts that played the Oasis: Dokken, Pat Travers, whoever. It was a great showcase room to play in front of those crowds. It was our Cavern. (That's a Beatles reference for all you kids.) The clubs we played were all eighteen and over to get in. Frank was too young to be in there, as he was still sixteen or seventeen. He'd have to sit in the back room between sets and come and go through the backstage door. That went on for about a year.

We wrote a lot of our first album during that period. In January 1985, Teresa Ensenat, an assistant A&R person at Geffen Records, had come out to see us open up for Montrose at the Crest Theatre because she liked the demo tapes we had done with Ronnie. We had a good set that night. We had some choreography going. Steve got us into better stage clothes, and with Troy in the band, we had gotten tighter for sure.

Teresa told us about her boss, Tom Zutaut, and then they scheduled time for us to go down and record at the Record Plant in LA with Duane. This was our second session with him. We did four songs—"I Know What I Need," "On the Run," "Curious Eyes," and "Headed for Disaster"—and Tom came to the sessions. At that time, he was leaving Elektra, where he'd signed Mötley Crüe and Dokken, to go to Geffen Records. We thought he was just jacking us off. He said, "You're not ready, you still have to write a lot of songs."

Tom didn't like Duane because he wimped the band out a bit, and Tom wanted us to be a rock band. It was actually the song "EZ Come EZ Go" that did Duane in. We had a version, the version we do now, and Duane changed it. He put in a "Cum On Feel the Noize" soccer-style chorus. Zutaut went mental and said, "That's it, he's going to ruin you, he's gotta go."

So Duane kind of fizzled out, which left the five of us making demos. Tom came over and started buying records by all these organic blues-based bands like Humble Pie, Bad Company, and UFO. He said, "Listen to this stuff, this is what you need to be doing." We're just coming off playing songs from *Pyromania* and *Blackout,* and Tom's saying, "You need to do a rootsy thing." He knew songs. On that first record he was very involved. He developed us for over a year and a half, from the time we signed in 1985 until our record came out at the end of 1986.

Everyone in our hometown said that we were full of shit, and we didn't have a record deal. But all through that time we were working with Tom and Teresa. Teresa was like Tom's mouthpiece. Tom would tell Teresa what we should be doing, and she would deliver the message. She got the demos first, and looking at it thirty years later, she saw us first, but Tom was the one who pulled all the strings.

Before we signed with Geffen, we had to fire Steve Clausman because of his unusual business practices. Steve was perfect for us when he started managing City Kidd. He taught us how to be hard workers and made us disciplined. He got us a place to practice and gigs to play. He brought in Ronnie and Duane to produce demos. He did a lot for us, but he just didn't know the music business. It's a cutthroat business. Record companies don't like to fuck around with beginners. They have to with the bands because they're the product. But when it comes to management and agents, not so much. Of course, when you do something like fire your manager, all the lawyers come out of the walls, and everything gets a little messy. Steve had expenses that we had to pay back, and his numbers didn't match our numbers. So we had all these lawsuits before we even signed anything. And we had to settle them before we could sign.

Now that we were getting signed, everyone was coming after us for money. Steve was cool; he just wanted to get paid and get his investment back. We had this lawyer, Mark Fleisher, that we hired to deal with Steve. And when we got Peter Paterno as a lawyer later on, Fleisher wanted part of our record deal because he figured we had gotten it on his watch. Steve came in to testify for us against Fleisher. It was kind of a trip. We never really fell out. When we fired him, before we even signed, we sat for a year and a half writing songs while this whole thing was going on. We had a few conference meetings in San Francisco. The first one he showed up in a suit and tie. We were all laughing at him, and he got mad. We're like "What the fuck's with you, dude, the suit and tie?" He got all bent out of shape. But the night we signed our contract, he rented a limo and drove us to our gig at the Oasis, because it was a feather in his cap. He wanted us to be successful, he just didn't know how to do it. But he can still say, "I developed them, I got them to that point." He did it.

What the Fuck's a Tesla?

Tom Zutaut had made his bones at Elektra, so to speak. We were his first signing at Geffen Records, which was a brand new label. At that time he was just working with us. We were the first record he had. We actually had the first successful rock record on Geffen. Aerosmith's *Done with Mirrors* came out before *Mechanical Resonance*, but it was a disappointment—I guess it was kind of done with mirrors. Our record came out, and it went platinum. Tom had gotten us to listen to the '70s British bands like Bad Company, Humble Pie, and Led Zeppelin. Those influences had a lot to do with us developing our own sound. Right after Tom finished our first album, he signed Guns N' Roses, and they went off the charts. We didn't see a lot of Tom after *Appetite for Destruction* hit it big.

Tom brought Cliff Burnstein in to see us at the Oasis, saying, "You gotta see this band." Cliff, who had signed Rush to PolyGram Records, really liked us. We loved Cliff because he had big crazy hair, a wild beard, and he looked like a homeless guy with this Tower Records bag he always carried to hold all his documents. That was a strange night because there was a historic flood in Northern

California, and our equipment truck got stranded in Stockton. We had to use another band's gear, but we didn't miss a beat.

I remember Cliff talking with us for about an hour after the show. He was a real musical guy; he was good with "that song needs a better chorus" kind of stuff. Cliff and Tom pretty much did A&R for Tesla's first two or three records. As things progressed over the years, Cliff did more A&R than Tom. In the beginning it was a lot of Tom with Cliff contributing, and by the second album kind of fifty-fifty, and *Psychotic Supper* was really Cliff's. Tom was off in Guns N' Roses heaven.

Tom said, "I can deliver you guys this manager," and he did. Cliff saw us and started working with us. So we signed our first record contract in June 1985, and for the next year all Tom and Cliff had us do was write songs. They wouldn't let us near a studio. Our team was Zutaut at Geffen as our A&R guy, and Cliff Burnstein and Peter Mensch as our managers.

We didn't meet Peter Mensch until we were mixing *Mechanical Resonance*. Cliff said he had this partner in England who was a legend over there and had signed and managed AC/DC. He also discovered Def Leppard. I didn't know who the fuck he was. We were in the last week or two of recording at Bearsville Studios when he came to Woodstock in upstate New York with Burnstein. I had this mental image of him being this old guy with a suit, and in walks this young dude wearing a T-shirt and jeans.

In the beginning, it seemed like Mensch didn't like us too much. We were more Burnstein's project. It wasn't until Mensch saw us play live on tour that he kind of got us. Burnstein got us from day one. I personally got on with Peter and still do to this day. He and I connected on a human level. I think Cliff is a genius, but he was all business. Cliff wasn't the kind of guy you could call and tell him your dog had died. He'd be, "Why are you calling me with this shit?"

Whereas I used to stay at Peter's house and go to baseball games with him. I still see him socially.

Getting back to making *Mechanical Resonance*, finding a producer was a chore, as almost everyone we contacted passed. We wanted Mutt Lange and Bruce Fairbairn, but they didn't want to do it. We approached Rick Rubin, and he said we weren't extreme enough. So, Tom brought in Chas Sandford, who wrote "Missing You" with John Waite, and Jim Faraci, who engineered Ratt's *Out of the Cellar* and had worked with L.A. Guns. We went into Cherokee Studios and cut six tracks—"Too Late For Love," "EZ Come EZ Go," "Changes," "Lil' Suzi," and "Better Off Without You"—but the demo came out like shit. Neither Chas nor Jim seemed to be in charge. They both had different ideas about how it should sound, and halfway through, Chas walked out. All the while, we're still writing songs.

After that they brought in Max Norman, who had worked with Ozzy Osbourne, Megadeth, and Bad Company. Max came to Sacramento and hung out for a couple of days. We partied and fucked some chicks. We got on fine, but, ultimately, he passed. The next guy we approached was Peter Collins. He had just produced "Out in the Fields" with Thin Lizzy bassist Phil Lynott, and also Rush, which was amazing. I remember we went out for this huge meal right before we played a showcase, so when we hit the stage we were all full and didn't play that well. I don't think Peter was that impressed by us, and he passed as well. Six years later, while producing my first wife's record in Louisiana, he said to me at dinner one night, "I should have done your record. I fucked up."

At that point Teresa sends me a record by Phantom, Rocker & Slick, who were the two sidemen from The Stray Cats with Earl Slick, who played guitar with David Bowie. It was produced by these New York guys, Steve Thompson and Michael Barbiero. Steve was a DJ, and Michael was an engineer who had worked on *Sesame Street* and a lot of remixes including "Harlem Shuffle" by The Rolling Stones.

They came out to see us, and they were about ready to pass. The story from Tom Zutaut goes that he literally got down on his knees and begged them to do our record and they agreed.

We were still writing and doing demos and had about half of a record. Tom, to his credit, would come up and hear what we had done. He came up one time and was furious because we hadn't written a song in three months. He threatened to drop us, and that scared the shit out of us. We went into this writing frenzy and wrote about twelve songs in two weeks, and half of those appeared on the album: "Modern Day Cowboy," "Gettin' Better," "Before My Eyes," "We're No Good Together," and "Cover Queen." It started to fall into place, and we went into rehearsals for two weeks.

Thompson and Barbiero were interesting cats. We didn't know how to take Steve. There were times in the past where I might have said that Steve wasn't that vital to the success of Tesla, but today I would say that I was absolutely wrong. Steve did things that you couldn't really see because he wasn't at the console messing with shit, and he wouldn't talk to you in musical terms. But in terms of dynamics, energy, and pumping you up, he was there. He was like, "I'm here for the vibe," and we thought that was kind of silly, and we actually dumped on him in interviews a couple of times, which I feel thoroughly bad about. When you're young, you don't realize that some of the things you say about people can be hurtful.

Another thing that came up during this time was that Steve and Michael didn't like Troy. Steve wanted to bring in Tony Thompson (Chic, David Bowie, Led Zeppelin post-John Bonham) to play drums on our record, and we were like, "No, we're not having any of that." I don't even think Troy knows that to this day.

Troy and I have had a lot of conflict over the years. Troy was the last guy to join Tesla, and he was older than us. If you look at the pictures of the guys in the band, we all look like we're in a rock band while Troy has got more of a conservative image. He had five kids. He joined the band with this chip on his shoulder. He's actually said to people in interviews that the band wouldn't have made it without him. Today we're OK, and I think we've both grown up, but there were times that he could be vicious with his mouth. I make no bones about the fact that Frank Hannon taught me how to play, and that when I first started, I wasn't a very good bass player. But the quality I had that Troy didn't see was that I'm the one who drives the band. I'm the one who made all the business contacts. Of course, today I think I play the bass pretty well, but fuck, I've been playing thirty-five years! On the first album I was no virtuoso, but rock bass players don't need to be virtuosos. The bass is there to support the music. When you have two guitar players who are both doing solos and a drummer who plays freely like Troy, someone must be solid and hold it down. I come from the school of Cliff Williams and Tom Peterson. Even though Paul McCartney's my favorite bass player, and I've learned to play like Paul over the years, that melodic style, I'm still very meat-and-potatoes. Troy has said some things in interviews on the history of Tesla, like when he first saw Jeff and Frank and they mesmerized him and that I still needed a lot of work to improve, which I don't think he realized wasn't the coolest thing to say 'cause it was hurtful.

We had to write and demo songs to get ready to make the first record. Generally, one of us would have a musical idea. Mostly it was Frank who would work on a music piece and then Jeff would write lyrics to it. I didn't really write too much. "Love Me" was the first complete song I wrote with Frank. I wrote part of "Cumin' at You Live," a couple of chords, little bits for "EZ Come EZ Go" and "Too Late for Love." Jeff always wrote lyrics to whatever music we had at that time. It wasn't until the second album when I started developing as a writer and wrote stuff like "Paradise." Now you can give me an idea about a guy who rows a canoe through the Amazon, and I'll write a song about it. That's developed over the years, but it wasn't like that in the beginning.

Frank would have a riff, then Tommy would play a riff, then they'd put together a piece of music, then we'd play it with the band. We'd record a demo on a little four-track recorder we had at that time, and then Jeff would write lyrics. That's kind of how it always went until the last couple of years.

The only part of the process that was painful was that it took Jeff a while to write lyrics, and we were impatient. Once we wrote the music, we expected lyrics the next day. He thought about it a lot, and he had to do whatever process he had to do to write them. I much prefer playing live, to be honest with you. The songwriting process with Tesla sometimes could be difficult and tedious.

We were always jockeying for songwriting credits. It made us competitive, and it inspired me to write so I could get some of my songs in the mix. There was a healthy competition between Frank and Tommy. Jeff just writes what he feels. He doesn't write in third person or in character, he writes about things that directly affect him.

Jeff's lyrics were pretty positive. There's no negativity. Jeff's a pretty positive guy. He always looks at the brighter, hopeful side. The one thing we did change when we were in Woodstock was Barbiero changed the chorus to "Modern Day Cowboy," and then Jeff kind of steered that. That wasn't the chorus we had originally. But that was a year-and-a-half process.

We went to Bearsville in the summer of 1986 to start making *Mechanical Resonance*. Bearsville was an amazing studio in Woodstock, New York, where there were a bunch of hippies living. You'd see people who maybe went out for a pack of cigarettes during the concert in 1969 (which actually took place in nearby Bethel) and think it's still going on. It was a great place to make a record. Four of us lived together while Troy lived at a different house. There was always this division between him and us. Troy was probably the biggest drug addict in the band until he got sober. Up until 1991 we would lose him for a couple of weeks at a time. When we made *The Great Radio Controversy*, after his drum tracks were done, we didn't see him until it was time for the photo shoot. He would be off doing a lot of cocaine. I only drank back then. I didn't do drugs until about 1993.

I think doing the record at Bearsville was Thompson and Barbiero's idea, partly because they were from that part of the country, and partly because Zutaut wanted us to go to a residence studio where we could live while recording. Thompson and Barbiero said there's this place in upstate New York that was a couple hours from their houses in New York, or New Jersey, wherever they were from. It was a legitimate studio. Cheap Trick, Foghat, and Todd Rundgren, among others, had recorded there. The Pretenders were there at the same time we were.

I think we were in rehearsal for two weeks, so we were there eight weeks total. It was like an old compound. It had a couple of houses and a cabin. Then there was this big place that looked like a barn that was the recording studio. We were there, and all we did was work on the album. We recorded in Studio A on a Neve desk that Bearsville got from The Who—a great console. It was an old desk from the '70s. We always recorded on Neves. The only things we ever did on an SSL (Solid State Logic) board before we got signed were the Hitchings demos and at Cherokee.

They didn't want us going into New York City, so what did we do the first weekend we had off? We rented a car and drove to Manhattan. We wanted to see Harlem. All five of us went, with Jeff driving. We had never been to New York. We were going through Manhattan, through Harlem, checking out the whole city. Jeff went up to the top of the World Trade Center. He also got ripped off by a cash machine for twenty dollars. Welcome to New York City. That was a great time. You only go the first time once!

Because Bearsville was a residence studio, there was a cook on the premises. She was a French woman named Martine. She would cook all this rich gourmet food. We said just give us the money, and we'll cook ourselves. That's what we did in Guam, so we knew how to use a stove. We were still into South Sacramento meat and potatoes. We hadn't discovered Thai food, or Vietnamese food, or Indian food. When we hit the road that would all change.

Most of the first album was just re-recording the arrangements we already had from doing all the different demos. "Getting Better," "Too Late for Love," "We're No Good Together," "Rock Me to the Top"—they were all the same. We just re-recorded them. But "We're No Good Together" and "Cover Queen," the jams in those songs might have been Steve's idea. Those were the kind of things that Steve did that I never even really thought about, like those jams. He didn't tell us what to play; he just said, "You gotta do something different here. We need to inject some energy here!" Frank put some big energy into the talk-box solo at the end of "Cover Queen."

We had a lot of fun making that album. In the early days there was a lot of support from the record company and the management; they were pretty hands-on. As we get deeper into the story, you will see how it waned after that. I suppose they were there when it counted, which was when we made that first record and turned the band into a brand. It certainly wouldn't have happened without Peter, Cliff, Tom, Teresa, Michael, and Steve. But when we finished laying down tracks, we were told by Cliff and Peter that we couldn't attend the mixes, which later on became a big resentment of ours. Their thinking was that we had never mixed a record, and we would get in the way and slow things down.

Mechanical Resonance was mixed at Media Sound in New York City, the same place we mixed *Great Radio Controversy*. When we finished tracking, we came home and started getting mixes from those guys. I didn't like the way it sounded. The guitars weren't loud enough. If you listen to that record, there's too much drum reverb, and Jeff's just buried in it. I don't remember if there was an EMT plate there, or what they were using for reverb, but there was a lot of it. It's certainly not as prevalent on *Great Radio Controversy*; it was toned down. It's still too much for my taste.

I guess Cliff and Peter didn't have a problem with it. They liked it, and it worked, so who am I to complain? All I can say is one day I'll take those tapes and remix them, and if it wasn't an issue with money or whatever, I'd love to do it with Thompson and Barbiero, and say, "Alright guys, let's redo this." We could do it at my studio for free. Just put it up, dump it into Pro Tools. But then you get into the whole thing that people want to get paid. I don't think I'd get anyone to cover the costs for us.

I think Troy has a copy of the master tape, but he can't remember where it is. I asked him about it because I would just go in and remix it. A couple of years ago, when we did the *Simplicity* album, we wanted to do it with Steve Thompson, and it just never worked out. We could never get the scheduling together, the budget together, whatever. Thompson and I had a couple of conversations, saying, "Wouldn't it be great to go back in and remix that first album?"

Back to the sessions. Funny thing was that unlike the mixing, we could be in the control room when tracks were being recorded. Michael would let you watch him mic up the drums, for example, and tell you what mics he was using and why. I didn't really get some of what he was saying, but later on, when I had my own studio, a lot of what he said came back to me.

I remember when Barbiero called me one time after sending a mix to review. He said, "Hey, did you get the mix of 'We're No Good Together?'"

I go, "Yeah."

He goes, "What'd you think of that chorus effect on the bass?"

I went, "What chorus?" I couldn't hear any chorus on the bass. I was like, "What are you talking about?" My criticism of that record is just that it's drenched in reverb. The reverb return is louder than the actual drums. I guess it was the style at that time, but fuck, Guns N' Roses, they didn't mix like that. And Guns N' Roses was at their mix sessions.

I think had we been there it would have been a little bit more in your face, the guitars especially. That was the bummer. We thought it was OK until we heard *Appetite for Destruction*, then we're like, "Well, fuck!" It was a lot punchier, and drier, and in your face. Axl's not buried in all the reverb they buried Jeff in, and to a degree they did that on *Great Radio Controversy* as well. It wasn't until we got to *Psychotic Supper* that I think there's a fair representation of what the band actually was supposed to sound like.

People in the industry and fans still come up to me and say, "*Mechanical Resonance* is a classic first record." I just hate the sound of it, and I don't think the other guys are particularly fond of it either. We could re-record it if we wanted to; there are no recording restrictions in our contract. But records are a snapshot of time in history, and you never finish a record, you just turn it in. *Mechanical Resonance* is an accurate snapshot of what was going on with Tesla in 1986. In hindsight, I'd like to have remixed it to the way all the rest of the records sound. Who knows? Maybe one day.

AT THE TIME OF RECORDING THE ALBUM we were still called City Kidd. Cliff and Tom (who had known each other since their early days in Chicago) said, "You gotta change your name. City Kidd sounds like Loverboy, that kind of pop band, and you're going to be a much rougher, tougher band." We'd sit around making up names.

Sometimes we'd sit around and talk to Chrissie Hynde of the Pretenders. She was real friendly to Jeff and me and would come up with some real vulgar names. She'd go, "Imagine this: 'Modern

Day Cowboy' by the new band, Dog's Balls!" I thought she was really cool. She's the kind of broad that if she had a dick, she'd pull it out and piss.

We'd almost finished recording and were about to mix the album, and Michael Barbiero had a barbecue at his house with his family. We're sitting at this cookout and Cliff says, "I've got an idea for a name for you guys—Tesla!"

So we're like, "What the fuck is that? It sounds like a black girl's name."

And he said, "Well, Nikola Tesla was this guy who invented all this stuff and never got credit for it and there's speculation as to whether the American government killed him." Cliff described Tesla as an underdog and equated it with rock 'n' roll, and we were like, "OK, we can wrap our heads around that."

A week later Tom flies out with this book on Tesla called *Man Out of Time*, gives each of us a copy, and tells us that he's going to have a quiz on it, and whoever gets all the questions right gets a hundred bucks. Tom was a good motivation guy! That's how the name Tesla came about. For the logo we brought in this guy, Nick Egan, and said, "Make the Tesla logo like the old RKO sign." I don't think anyone ever got that hundred bucks, by the way.

Frank came up with the album title. He said, "Oh there's this chapter, Mechanical Resonance. It was a theory Nikola Tesla had that everything has a resonant frequency and that the earth has a mechanical resonance, and if you turned that tone up loud enough, you could split the earth and blow it up." That was the idea behind the album. Our songs were going to blow up, and we were going to step on the scene and be this band with this whole new thing. Frank came up with the title *The Great Radio Controversy*, too. Frank is a creative motherfucker!

Troy got really into it and started this whole campaign of getting the bust of Nikola Tesla in the Smithsonian museum in

Washington, DC. I didn't really give a fuck, to be honest. It was like, we couldn't come up with a name, Cliff and Tom told us a name, and we went "OK." And that gave us something to talk about at interviews. I personally was never really a Tesla trumpeter. You can't put too much into that name, because if we were called Club Sandwich, the songs would have been the same. We still would have been those guys from broken homes, and the story of the band and the music would have been the same. It just conveniently tied itself into this crazy scientist, and maybe if you believe in God and cosmic destiny and all that shit, then maybe it was it was meant to be. I'd like to believe that it was kind of meant to be, because I'm a spiritual guy. But Tesla wasn't a name we picked. We didn't come in there like Joe Elliott, who drew "Def Leppard" in his song book. He picked that name. We couldn't come up with one. Tom and Cliff can take credit for it; I don't know who really did. I somehow think it was Cliff to be honest. Cliff was a pretty intellectual guy. Cliff would know about him. Cliff looked like he could have been a fuckin' mad scientist!

I don't think we would have gone back to Earthshaker either. Tesla's as cool a name as any name. Especially with the car now, people really know the name; they know more of the car now than they do us, which is kind of a shame because we did it twenty fuckin' years before that car ever came out and had two top-ten singles. It kind of bums me out sometimes, but I've reached out to Elon Musk, and we kind of communicate back and forth through his assistant. He knows of us, and we know about him. We sent him some Tesla shirts because we saw a picture of him wearing one of our shirts, and he sent us some car shirts. That's all cool. It gave us something to talk about in interviews.

Many kids today know who Nikola Tesla is, and I'd like to think that we had something to do with that. That was probably in the back of Cliff, Peter, and Tom's minds when they chose the name. It was nothing to do with us; we wouldn't have picked that name in a million years, now it rolls off the tip of your tongue. But if you've never heard it, it's like "What the fuck's a Tesla?" Now we've met all kinds of kids named Tesla.

After one show, at a meet-and-greet, a guy came up to me and said, "Hey man, I named my son after you."

I said, "That's cool, I haven't met many boys called Tesla."

He said "No, I named him Brian Wheat!"

I was like, "OK, security!"

The Tomato Farmers
from Sacramento

Up until the time we made *Mechanical Resonance* I was the fat kid. I topped out at 250 pounds at 5'8". The free food I got from working at McDonald's is what started me down that path. Growing up poor, I never got McDonald's; that was considered a real big treat. I've been known to go into a supermarket and spend two hundred dollars on sweets. I do that because when I was a kid, I didn't have any. I live in a big house because when I was a kid, I lived in a tiny house. That's the psychology behind who I've become. I also saved a lot of money, which was instilled in me by my mother. She said, "You should save half of everything you make." She had to stretch dollars to feed all of us.

The first time I met Peter Mensch, he said to me, "You're going to do a photo session with this famous photographer, don't worry about being fat. I'll tell him to put you at the back of the photo and tell everybody you're not the lead singer." Then he smiled at me with his big teeth. That really hit me. He was brutal. And I realized that he wasn't the only one on me about it. I knew this was a crucial point in my career...my life. I had a shot at playing rock 'n' roll for a living. I'm sure it weighed on the band's minds. I'm sure there were people at Geffen who were ready to have me replaced. Image is a huge thing, and looking like I did just wasn't going to cut it. I could wind up like Brook and Bobby, kicked to the curb. So when I came home after making that record in September, Peter didn't see me until we did a tour with David Lee Roth. I went on a diet and lost eighty pounds.

It was called the Rotation Diet. It was something I found at a local grocery store called Raley's. The idea was that you had 800 calories one day, then 1100 the next, 1400 the third day, then repeat the whole thing. My mom cooked for me and prepared all my meals. I was living with Buddy, but I'd go home to eat. She bought a scale and got a good measuring cup, and that's the amount I would eat, no seconds! I think it was about four months, and then the weight started dropping off fast, and when I lost about thirty pounds, I started playing racquetball and running six miles a day at the Hiram Johnson track. Once you get that metabolism going, it's nothing. I couldn't run one fuckin' lap around the track when I started, then later I was running half-marathons.

Oddly, but helpfully, exercising at this level started knocking the edges off the anxiety that I'd always had. But on the downside, years of running on hard surfaces like streets and sidewalks have fucked up my feet, and I have heel spurs pretty bad, so now I just ride my elliptical bike. I never really learned the warm-up routines either, I'd just take off running. I hurt my Achilles tendon one time running a race in cold weather because I didn't warm up properly.

Losing the weight taught me that everyone has the power to control what they need to do. Personally, it was just sheer discipline. There was nothing fun or enjoyable or easy about it when I first started. But when the goal is in sight, it gets a lot easier, and you feel good about yourself. Attaining that goal shows you that it's possible. Then you can start to think that way about other things in your life: relationships, career, whatever. It's willpower and perseverance. That's the formula. It got me there where I needed to be.

We all get lazy at times or we don't care, but that's not an excuse. That's the key. Don't make excuses because they're easy to find. I think of myself like a car. Nobody wants an ugly car. I'm a public personality: a commodity. Fans look up to us, many of them would trade places with us in a heartbeat. It's partially a false image. We've got the same issues as most people. They're just magnified because we're in the public eye. That's why you have to present that enviable image. That's what the fans want.

Cliff Burnstein didn't recognize me when I walked past him twice at the Newark airport. That was all the result of Peter Mensch. That's what I respect about Peter to this day. He puts people off because he's blunt. When Peter said that about my weight, I just left thinking, "I'll show you, you cocksucker!" That's how I got the nickname Shredded Wheat because then I became Mensch's hero. The guys in Def Leppard knew about me before I ever met them. Steve Clark told me that he admired me for overcoming my weight problem. Maybe he equated it with what he was going through with alcohol at the time. Keeping the weight off was relatively easy for me, at least compared to losing it, because I was very active. Between playing on most nights while touring and exercising every day, I burned enough calories that I just had to avoid bingeing to maintain my weight. I really became obsessed with my weight. Chicks were paying attention to me now. They actually wanted me! That was just a mind blower. I'd never had that before. There was no way I was gonna go back to being the fat kid in the back. I had a scale on the road, and I'd measure out portions, just like my mom did. If I put on a couple of pounds, I just wouldn't eat until those pounds came off. And until 1998 I kept the weight off. When I wasn't exercising as much as I should have been, I'd stick my fingers down my throat after a meal and puke it up. I actually became borderline bulimic for a while from doing that.

I struggle with my weight now because of the medication I take for my autoimmune disease. I've learned to accept it a bit more. But it doesn't matter. I'm not the lead singer, and I'm not trying to create a brand. When you're young and trying to break into the business, you've got to be good looking, have great songs, and a great live show.

The famous photographer that Peter was talking about was Ross Halfin. At the time he was *the* guy. He was shooting everybody. He'd done the UFO stuff that we liked, and he was really good friends with Peter, so he was doing Def Leppard: portraits, live shots, everything. He was the tour photographer, studio photographer, did the album covers, press photos. We did our very first photo shoot with him in New York when we were finishing up *Mechanical Resonance*, before we started mixing it. We thought he was a dick. Everyone in the band couldn't stand him.

We did the shoot in the Meat District in the back of a meat truck. This black hooker comes over to us, and she's wearing a nightgown and holding her tit. She looks at Ross, squeezes her tit, and milk comes out. He screams at her, "Get out of here, you skank."

And she says, "I'll suck all y'all's dicks for fifteen dollars," as she's sticking her tongue out. And we're freaked out because we're just kids, and here's this crazy English guy with this crazy accent who's rude to everybody. And a lactating prostitute as well. It's a pretty funny picture: Jeff's got long hair, and I've got fat cheeks; my head is like a basketball. This is the shoot during which Mensch told me to stand at the back. Ross has since embellished the story saying that some of the band had a go with the hooker, which is bullshit.

We went back to Peter and said, "We don't like that guy. We don't ever want to take photos with him again."

And Peter said, "He's just that way. The next time you do a shoot, just yell back at him. Tell him to fuck off." So we did. Eventually when we went to England, we saw a lot of him, and that's how Ross and I built up our friendship. He's one of my best friends now. And people still think he's an asshole. What's funny is that we've only really started using his pictures in the last few years.

Mechanical Resonance ended up going multiplatinum. The first single we released was "Modern Day Cowboy," and as soon as that came out on radio and then the video got played on MTV, *bang*! All the stations started adding it to their rotations.

At that time, the Russians had shot down a Korean airliner, killing 270 people. And there was that cold war tension between us. Then you had the Olympics in the USSR, which we boycotted; all that was still pretty fresh. That was a Frank and Tommy composition, and Jeff was telling me about the lyrics one day driving down to Stockton to rehearse. He said something about modern day cowboys playing cowboys and Indians, kind of like Russia and the US, and that made for the storyboard. It was pretty clever. The first thing people saw about us wasn't in hot tubs with chicks. It was good timing.

We didn't have any input on the "Cowboy" video. They plopped us on a stage in an empty theater, and we just played the song over and over. The makeup people gave us ratted and sprayed hair. They tried that for "Cowboy" and "Lil' Suzi," and that was the end of that. That didn't work. We went along with it on the first two videos. "Suzi" was the real awful one. Ratted-out hair and extreme close-ups. Just horrible. We were like, "Fuck that, we're not doing that again." So the next video, which was "Gettin' Better," was really stripped down and workmanlike. We did it in Pennsylvania, played in a little club, and that was the end of the hairspray for us. This isn't Poison or Mötley Crüe. Nothing against those bands; I toured with both of them, and I liked both of them, but Tesla is a different kind of animal, more like Bad Company. If you look at Axl Rose in the video for "Welcome to The Jungle," you can see they did the same thing to him! It was just cookie-cutter marketing.

The record came out in November, and we sat around until February. For three years we had played and rehearsed in Sacramento, then Tom signed us and was developing us, and then we put out this record and it went to radio. It got thirteen adds its first week, and the next week it got forty. It's snowballed, and the next thing you know we're on tour in front of ten thousand people a night. David Lee Roth was going on tour at the time with his first solo album, *Eat 'Em and Smile*. The story is that he got a list of videos from MTV of young bands, and he brought his crew in to watch them. He asked, "Which of these bands do you guys like?"

The crew all liked "Modern Day Cowboy" and Roth said "OK, that's who we're taking." Maybe the hairspray in the video was a good thing!

Mechanical Resonance shot up the charts, and we were on tour with David Lee Roth. We were blown away that people knew who we were. It was like overnight. We went from playing six-hundred-seaters as City Kidd to our first gig as Tesla at New Haven, Connecticut, in front of twelve thousand people. They just threw us out to the lions. We kind of had it together, and when they put us on that big stage, it wasn't completely alien. We did well because the Oasis had a pretty big stage. We had this crew guy, Dan McClendon, who used to be in the back, lighting smoke bombs, fire pots, and shit. We used to take all these lights in there, and we'd do mini-concerts. We had watched the Scorpions and Def Leppard, and saw how they jumped around, so we did all that. We were imitating what we'd seen.

It was louder than the clubs for sure. We had a wall of Marshall stacks, and the arenas just sucked up the volume, so we had to turn everything up just to hear ourselves. Back then there were no in-ear monitors, so the floor wedges and side fills added even more volume to the stage. I don't think we got one sound check on the entire tour.

Dave Lee Roth was fine. He did some stuff that was kind of funny. Like if he was walking down the hallway, you had to duck into a room and get out of his way. We were green at the time, but I wouldn't put up with that kind of shit after that tour. But he talked to us a couple of times. After a show in Lakeland, Florida, his security guy, Eddie Anderson, called us and said, "Dave wants to see you now!" So we went up to his room, and he's got two chicks with him, and there are panties on the floor. It looked kind of like a setup. I don't know if he was trying to impress us. He's got this big bag of cocaine, a long fingernail on his pinkie, and he's snorting blow. He's playing this whole Diamond Dave thing and starts giving us a rap about doing interviews and then he just comes out with, "Me and Pete [Peter Angelus, Roth's manager] want to manage you. We think you're great."

And we say, "Well, we have managers."

And he said, "We don't care, we want to manage you." We were flattered. We sent him a gold record and have never spoken to him since. Having said that, the band and crew were great and really looked out for us. David was cool, but the rock-star stuff was weird. Billy Sheehan, the bass player, and Gregg Bissonette, the drummer, were pretty cool to us. Steve Vai was kind of standoffish; he had this guitar-hero trip kind of going on. Replacing Eddie Van Halen, right?

Being on tour was a big party, like going to Disneyland. I'd get up at noon or so, eat breakfast and work out, maybe go do a record-store appearance or a radio interview, go back to the venue, and get ready for the gig. After our set I'd pull a chick and have some sex, drink, get on the bus, go in the back lounge, turn off all the lights and listen to Motown, or Zeppelin, or whatever we were listening to back there until we passed out. Then do it again the next day. We were in a different city every day—Charlotte, Nashville,

Chicago, Denver, Boston, Houston, Miami, wherever. The lifestyle was coming at me a hundred miles an hour, I was just trying to take it in. We were doing five shows a week.

We made friends with David Lee Roth's wardrobe person, Robin Lemon, and she did our laundry for us. Until we were headliners, we'd just slide the headline staff a few bucks, and they would take care of it. That was pretty typical. Our own crew was minimal at that point. Dan, whom I mentioned earlier, was the stage-right tech. Then we had a stage-left tech for Frank, a drum tech, a sound guy, and our road manager, Nigel James.

We started seeing our fan base grow right out of the gate on that first tour. It was only six weeks, but we saw a lot of our fans in the audiences during that time—meet-and-greets, in-stores, that kind of thing. People were really digging our album and live show. Somebody branded us "America's Band," and in a lot of ways it made sense. We had big followings in the Northeast and Florida, but we got pretty huge throughout the rust belt. I think it's just because of the way people live their lives. I think it's the message in our songs. We're normal Americans. A lot of it is Jeff because people relate to lyrics. If we were an instrumental band, people wouldn't care. I've told everyone that without Jeff there's no Tesla. But that's with any band. They always identify with the singer. If something happened to Jeff, if he quit, would I want to go on with some guy like the dude that took Steve Perry's place in Journey? I don't know.

Where we never have done really great has been on the West Coast. LA has always been hit or miss, San Diego too. We do OK in Seattle and Portland now. There was a time Seattle wasn't too friendly. But the place that meant the most was New York City. As soon as we got there, which was the third gig, there were people who said, "I love your record, I came to see you guys." People in the music industry as well. Someone asked Nikki Sixx about Tesla when our first album came out, and he said "Oh, those guys, they're tomato farmers from Sacramento, right?"

After the David Lee Roth tour, we sold about three hundred thousand records in a couple of months, and the next tour was with Alice Cooper for six weeks. That just kind of popped up, so there wasn't much time between Roth and Alice. It wasn't like the Roth tour. The arenas were half-full, and we were playing in B-markets. You'd walk in, and the upper level of the arena would be curtained off. But it was a good experience for us, as we were still honing our live show and getting better. We filled up days with record-store appearances and interviews at radio stations. We were up for any type of promotion. We were very hungry.

The schedule was tighter too. Alice would often do six shows a week. He was a hard worker. That was OK, it was one more payday and one day less a week that we had to pay for hotel rooms. Unfortunately, like the Roth tour, we didn't get many sound checks.

Alice was a nice guy. The entire star-trip, pretentious shit was out the window. Alice didn't make you get out of the way if he was walking down the hall. He didn't have any of this heavy groupie scene on his tour, so that left all the chicks for us. Vince is a cool guy except for when he puts on the makeup and becomes Alice! Then he was in character, and you didn't want to try any small talk or anything. We didn't see him much, to be honest with you. You wouldn't see him at the gigs hanging out or anything. We knew his band and hung out with them, but you didn't really see Alice much. Never really had a serious conversation with him. Not because he didn't want it, it was just he was a private guy.

Alice didn't do sound checks. The band would do them; he didn't. He'd just come and do the show, then split and go to his own bus. I think he was sober at the time, coming off of the '70s when he was all wild and shit. It wasn't like he was hanging out. But I've seen him a few times over the years. He's come to our gigs in Phoenix.

Peter Mensch came out to visit when we were with Alice, and he had come out a little bit when we were with David Lee Roth. Peter was the guy who would come out for a day or two. Cliff wasn't really into that. He would stay in the office. Cliff came to the last David Lee Roth show, in Lakeland, Florida. Kind of an end-of-the-tour thing. But he came. Peter would actually ride on the bus with us, and we would talk about things. Peter was my buddy. He always critiqued the band; you should do this, do that. We should have listened to him more. Some things we did listen to, some things we didn't. Cliff and Peter were real involved in the beginning. We just wore them out and were more trouble than we were worth because we didn't listen.

Peter and Cliff's company was called Q Prime. In the '80s they were managing Def Leppard, Metallica, Queensrÿche, and Dokken. We weren't selling the numbers those other bands were, so they weren't prepared to take our bullshit, because the money wasn't warranting it. But Peter and Cliff loved Tesla.

I remember Peter thinking we were a great live band. I think what impressed him was that we could play together live and sound like our records. Our records were not as polished as Leppard's ever were, and maybe that's why he wasn't that crazy about how the records sounded. Maybe that's why he didn't like our first album. He liked the second album. Now he thinks the first album is a classic. Funny how time and success can alter one's point of view.

The Roth tour was six weeks, the Alice tour was six weeks, and I think we did four weeks on our own in clubs. Back then you could play like fifteen shows in Texas. We played some small clubs and stuff on our own. And then we wound up, I think the last show on that run was the Texas Jam with Boston, Aerosmith, Whitesnake, and Poison.

After that we went out with Def Leppard. We were just waiting for the right time for that to come up, waiting for them to finish their album. Leppard was coming off a four-year break. When we signed with Peter and Cliff, the first thing we asked them was, "Can you get us on the Def Leppard tour?"

They said, "Well, we'll try, it's up to the band." That tour just busted us wide open. But it really started earlier, because of MTV and David Lee Roth and the radio all at one time.

When we were in Earthshaker, we wanted to be Def Leppard. I saw them open up for Pat Travers in 1980 on their first tour for *On Through the Night*. Then, in 1981, Frank and I went to see them tour *High 'n' Dry*, opening for Blackfoot. I met Pete Willis and Rick Allen that night. Somehow, my buddy Terry Muñoz and I were out by their bus, and Terry said, "Hey, I got some pot."

Rick Allen said, "Well look, we're staying at the Holiday Inn, on Forty-Seventh off of Ninety-Nine. Would you come over?" So we drove over there and hung out with them and smoked weed. I tell Rick about that, and he says he remembers, but he doesn't. He's just being nice about it. But I remember. Five years later we were fuckin' opening up for Def Leppard!

When Leppard was finally done making *Hysteria*, Peter Mensch played us a few of the tracks: "Women," "Hysteria," and "Rocket." We loved "Women" and said, "That's the fuckin' single, man!" Later on, Mensch told us that Frank and I were the reason they chose it as their first single.

Prior to the Leppard tour, we were in Europe doing some shows on our own including Montreux, Düsseldorf, Amsterdam, and two shows at the Marquee in London. People in England liked us because we were a blues-based rock band with English influences like Bad Company, Led Zeppelin, and Humble Pie. It was great.

When Leppard finally finished *Hysteria*, Cliff and Peter got us on their tours of the US and UK. Joe Elliott was a bit standoffish in England. I hung out a lot with Steve Clark. I remember one night we were in the bar, Jeff Keith came in and Steve gave him a hundred dollars and told him to take his wife out to dinner. He was a really generous guy. I just used to sit there and get shitfaced with him. I remember one night we were sitting at a bar in a really nice hotel in Manchester, and the bartender refused to sell us any more booze because we had already sunk two bottles of Jack Daniel's. So we went up to Steve's bedroom and started jumping up and down on the mattress, throwing shapes and posing, imitating Jimmy Page, because Steve worshipped Led Zeppelin. I go back to my room and jump into the shower because I'm so fucked up, I'm scared that I'm going to end up like John Bonham. The next thing you know, I'm wandering around the hotel corridors butt-ass naked looking for Dan McClendon. I end up knocking on the door, and it's fucking Peter Mensch!

When we got to America, the tour started off to half-full houses. Like Alice Cooper, the upper levels were draped off. We did six months, and it gradually kept getting bigger and bigger because of the singles they were releasing. Joe would get really discouraged, and I remember I kept saying to Phil Collen, "As soon as you release 'Love Bites,' this record is going to be really fucking massive!" By this time *Mechanical Resonance* had gone platinum, and we're playing in the round; it was a big thing. We were young, and we didn't have anything, no cars or houses. I was still living in Buddy's spare room. But I was now partying every night, fucking chicks, and playing rock 'n' roll. Every night was Friday night, and it couldn't get better than that!

The Def Leppard tour had a lot to do with Tesla becoming big. The David Lee Roth tour took us from zero to three hundred thousand albums sold. The next million records came from being on tour with Def Leppard. When the tour got to America, I bonded with Joe Elliott. We went into Glens Falls, New York, for three days' rehearsal, and Frank and I had a room next to Joe. He must have heard us playing music, because he knocked on the door and said,

"What are you guys up to?" So I invited him in. We started jamming on all these Paul McCartney songs, because Joe's a big Wings fan. We became good buddies really quick. What I didn't realize was that this was the night Steve Clark tried to break his hand by punching it into the wall because he didn't want to go on tour. So Joe was probably troubled by that, and that's why he came over and hung out with us.

When I met Steve Clark, I was a kid; I didn't know he had a problem. I didn't know what a drug and alcohol problem was. This was his way of life; he just liked to have a drink, and I didn't realize that it was so out of control. I did later. I saw him two weeks before he died. There was a lot of sex and drugs in the early days, but we've never really talked about it compared to bands like Mötley, Guns N' Roses, and Poison. We always talked about the music, which was the thing with Tesla. If you saw Jeff Keith walking down the street at the height of our career, you probably wouldn't know who he was because we're not an image band.

We've only had one cover story in the whole of our career until last year. Even though we were on MTV a lot of the time, we were never at the VMA awards. We had the number one song on MTV in '91, which was "Signs"; they didn't even ask us to come to the VMAs. And I think that was because there was no Steven Tyler or Angus Young in our band. At the height of our career when we were playing arenas, I used to walk around the venue when the opening band was on, and no one even knew that it was me.

On the last day of the tour in El Paso, Texas, the Leppard guys came to our dressing room and gave us portable four-track recorders and said, "We want you to go and write a great second album." So I guess they looked at us as their young protégés and they were mentoring us. Joe Elliott always was and still is a big mentor to me in my musical life.

We went away to write and gave Joe our demos. "Party's Over" went on *The Great Radio Controversy* because Joe liked it so much. Cliff and Peter didn't like it, but we said, "No, you've got to put it on because Joe likes it." It's a piece of shit song, actually. Joe is one of my best friends to this very day.

When my studio burned down, he phoned me and said, "If you need any gear, Def Leppard will loan you a back line, anything." No one else in the music business reached out to me like that. There's a definite kinship between us. He's Fat Bastard One, I'm Fat Bastard Two.

One of the things I wanted to do when we got to England was meet Paul McCartney. I knew that Mensch was a friend of Richard Ogden's, McCartney's manager, and I asked him if he could arrange a meeting. Peter said, "I ain't fucking doing that. Why would Paul McCartney want to meet some kid in a band that I'm managing who doesn't mean anything?"

I thought, "Fuck you! I'll do it myself!" So I'm at Geffen's London office with Frank Hannon one day, and we're walking through Soho Square, and opposite Geffen's office is MPL (McCartney's office). I look up on the third floor, and there's Paul McCartney standing at the window, looking like he's smoking this big joint. I said "Frank! There's fucking Paul McCartney!" He sees me and I give him the thumbs-up, and he gives me the thumbs-up back. I pointed at him and made a gesture like, "Can you come down and take a picture?" He looked back and held up all ten fingers.

Ten minutes later he comes out of the building and I'm shaking. We take a photo, and I say nervously, "Hi I'm in a band and we've come over from America and my first record is out and we're playing the Marquee."

And he said, "Oh, that's great, lots of people started there." He was really nice, polite, and courteous, and I took five shots with him. Frank fucked off and went to look at guitars.

The next day we played Amsterdam, and Peter was there with Leppard, and he took Phil Collen, Steve Clark, and Richard Allen down to the show. We worked it out where we had a jam at the end of the night playing "Rock of Ages," and there's a clipping somewhere that says Def Tesla. They were great to us and took us out partying for the night. Phil was sober by then, but Steve definitely wasn't. Anyway, at the sound check I see Peter and shout out, "Peter, come here, I got something to show you!" He comes over and I pull out a folder of these photos of me and McCartney. Mensch just grabs me, gives me a kiss, and says, "Man, you've got balls the size of Texas."

The second time I met McCartney was backstage at Arco Arena in Sacramento, 2002. I was with our wardrobe person, Ali Amato, backstage. She had been with Tesla from *Great Radio Controversy* to *Bust a Nut*. In 2002 she was working for McCartney. Paul just walked in and said, "Who's your friends, Ali?"

"This is Brian and Monique."

He said "Hi, I'm Paul."

We said, "We know who you are!" He was checking my wife Monique out, and I said, "I play bass in a band called Tesla."

He said, "Ah, cool."

I said, "I play a Hofner like you."

"Ah, great, are you the singer?"

"No, I don't sing, no."

I know his drummer who played on "Live and Let Die," and "My Love," and all the records up to "Band on the Run," Denny Seiwell. And Denny's wife is named Monique as well. So I was telling Paul I saw Denny, and he said, "Oh yeah, I saw Denny the other day, he came to the show in LA," and he went, "Monique, that's Denny's wife, cool, man." Again, he was really nice. I was kind of freaked out, as I wasn't expecting him to walk in. We were just hanging out in wardrobe with Ali. It wasn't a meet-and-greet thing. He just walked in to see her about something.

Sophomore Jinx?

When we made the first album, Tesla was just a band that played clubs around Sacramento. On *The Great Radio Controversy*, we were a band that had toured the world. We were essentially rock stars now. We weren't Def Leppard, but people knew who Tesla was. We had more confidence going into the second record and even a growing attitude of ego and arrogance. We finished touring to support *Mechanical Resonance* and started writing songs. There wasn't much of a break.

There wasn't much writing before the end of the Leppard tour. Maybe Frank had some ideas. Frank always experimented with recorders at home and stuff. I hadn't started anything yet. We moved into a rehearsal room in West Sacramento and spent six, seven months just writing and recording demos. That's what became the second album. No holdovers from previous writing sessions; the second album was all new material.

We did the demos on an eight-track that Frank had gotten. We each brought in whatever stuff we had from the four-tracks that Leppard gave us and worked it out in the warehouse and then laid it down to eight-track. We gave that to Jeff, and he put the lyrics together over the next few months. He wrote all the lyrics on *Controversy*. Then we'd mix those down to cassettes and send them off to Peter, Cliff, and Tom.

They liked some of the stuff. The funny thing was that all three of them did *not* like "Love Song." We had to fight to put that on the album. We always reminded them of that when they disagreed with us. So we kept writing songs and also fit in some dates with Def Leppard, who by then were massive. Then Steve Thompson and Michael Barbiero joined us, and we went back up to Bearsville. We were there much longer this time, as there would be a lot more production on this record.

There was definitely a maturity in the second album. When we wrote and recorded the first album, we had never played in an arena. When we made the second album, we'd played the Texas Jam, we'd played all these sold-out shows with Def Leppard all over the world. We knew what it was like to be a live band, so there was a lot more conviction. We knew we wanted it to sound bigger. The first album was done on one twenty-four-track machine, and the second album was done on two twenty-four-tracks synced up. It was a lot more produced.

Bearsville had forty-eight tracks available when we did the first album, but Tom had a vision of us as a raw, almost live-to-tape kind of band, so *Mechanical Resonance* only used one 24-track machine. But, as I said, we were growing some healthy egos coming off our success, so this time we laid down demands; we wanted forty-eight tracks, we wanted to spend more time laying down tracks, double the guitar tracks, and we wanted to be present at the mixes. We were a lot better prepared coming into these sessions. Our arrangements were locked down, we were confident and experienced. Steve and Michael really just rolled tape when we were tracking.

The record was called *The Great Radio Controversy* because there was a controversy about who invented the radio; was it Marconi or Tesla? In the schoolbooks we were taught it was Marconi, but that patent has been since overturned by the Supreme Court, and it's been handed back over to Tesla. "Heaven's Trail" was the first single we released. Then it was "Hang Tough," "Love Song," and "The Way It Is." All those songs were very different from each other, which for us was a good thing. A lot of bands would just repeat a successful formula over and over, but we wouldn't, or maybe couldn't, do that. *The Great Radio Controversy* is bigger sounding than *Mechanical Resonance*, but there's less reverb; the sound came more naturally.

What we figured out on the second record is that we didn't work for Geffen Records or Q Prime, they worked for us. So we brought a lot of that attitude: "Now you're dealing with a band that's had a multiplatinum-selling album, people adore us." We began to assert ourselves. One time, Tom came to the studio, and they had bunch of food, and I came in and ate his crackers. He said something to me about it and I said, "Well, fuck it! We paid for them anyway."

Because I realized every time the record company took you out to dinner, they stuck it on your bill. They're taking us out to all these extravagant meals, flying us to the Sunset Marquis. You're thinking that David Geffen is the greatest guy in the world, and it ends up that we're paying for all of it, and we didn't know it! We started to realize this when we got our royalty statements. We sold a million and a half records, and we're not making much money? What's going on?

Well, we have to pay back the album budget, all the photo sessions, hotels, and travel. We had to pay for all the videos we made, even though we had no say in how much those videos cost, or how they would look, or anything. Because we were only touring as an opening act, we weren't making shit on the road either. So there was money that Geffen chipped in as tour support, and that had to be paid back as well. Our tour bus cost five hundred dollars a day. Plus, when we got signed, we had an old lawyer we had to fire, along with Steve Clausman and Duane Hitchings, and they had to get paid off from the first album. We soon found out that we were the last guys to get paid. We weren't paying attention to what was being spent; we thought there was tons of money everywhere. Like us, a lot of young bands nowadays don't realize that. We weren't making that kind of dough. They way Peter and Cliff put it was, "You want to see some money, write some hits." Other than that, they didn't really talk about money to us.

There was a relatively small, but significant event that happened early in 1989 on tour. Up until then we had existed on advances from record sales and per diems when we were on the road. One day we all received checks for several thousand dollars. It took a minute to realize that this was money from actual sales, not advances. Anyway, Tom and I sorted out the thing with the crackers, we kissed and made up. He's a really good guy.

Tesla had more confidence now. *No* was not in our vocabulary from the second album on. Unfortunately, there were times people told us no when we should have listened.

As we're recording the album, there are no fights or anything, but we're starting to wonder what role it is that Steve Thompson is fulfilling. On the first album Michael was the engineer, and he could talk to you in music terms, and Steve could talk to you in terms of dynamics. We didn't really understand the difference between the two, which I do now. So there was a little bit of friction between Steve and us at times.

Aside from wanting to record more tracks, Jeff said, "I want to sing more like me—naturally," because they had him singing a lot deeper on the first record. We were taking a bit of control. All the things that we had resented from the first record, we fixed on the second.

We mixed *Controversy* at Media Sound in New York. Frank and I stayed for the mixes this time. We were just being assertive. We didn't get aggressive until the next studio record, *Psychotic Supper*.

The first Tesla song I had anything to do with writing was "Love Me" on the first album. Frank and I did that in his garage studio back in 1985. He played drums, and I played guitar. We just built it out of a jam. On *Controversy* I wrote part of "Makin' Magic," "Flight to Nowhere," the bass intro on "Hang Tough," and the B section on "Lady Luck." The song "Paradise" was a bit of a struggle. It was my first song that I wrote from scratch, and there was some resistance from Frank and Tommy. It was also a new process for me because I wrote it on piano, and that might have had something to do with the resistance. It wasn't going to be a typical Tesla guitar song.

I had gotten this old upright piano from Virgil McKenzie, the keyboardist from 58 Fury, a Sacramento band that Steve Clausman was managing. "Paradise" is a very McCartney-esque song. Think of "You Never Give Me Your Money," the first song of the B-side medley on Abbey Road. And Queen, they were a big influence on me. Tom Zutaut loved that song. I wrote it at Buddy's house. I actually prefer the version of "Paradise" on Five Man Acoustical Jam. It's more spare and feels more appropriate to me. I think for the studio recording I was going for a "Bohemian Rhapsody" thing, to get a big dynamic buildup, lots of guitars in the B section. But it may have been overproduced, so I prefer the live version now.

IT WAS DURING THIS TIME THAT I MET MY FIRST WIFE. I left Bearsville to go to New York for about three weeks for the mix sessions. One weekend I drove back to Bearsville to play some mixes for Ian, the guy who ran the studio. There was a band there called Saraya mixing their album, who were named after their singer—Sandi Saraya. The people at the studio introduced me to Sandi; I thought she was beautiful. She's a beautiful woman to this day. Sandi said, "I really like Mechanical Resonance."

I said, "Uhhh, thanks," because at that time I was really uncomfortable taking praise from people, but she took it as me being kind of stuck up. So I invited her to have a listen to some new mixes, and she played me a couple of songs from her record. I said, "Give me your address, and I'll send you a copy of the record when it's done." I didn't ask her for a phone number because I was too shy.

Six months later, in 1989, I was in Orlando, Florida, touring with Poison. One of the radio promotion guys picked me up, and I asked him what he'd been working on. He said, "Oh, I got this girl down in Daytona named Sandi Saraya."

I said, "I know her." It was, *Flash! Boom!*

When we got to New Jersey with Poison, I checked New Jersey information to see if I could find her number. But her real last name was Salvador. It turned out her middle name was Saraya. So I was never able to contact her, and I never sent her a CD because I lost the piece of paper with her address.

Now she's in Florida, where I was the day before. And when she checked into her hotel room, it turned out to be the same room I was in the night before, and there's a note there for me from radio IDs I had done. She's trippin' out on that, thinking, "Wow, that's the dude from Tesla," and I'm three hundred miles away in another city thinking about this girl I met in Bearsville. That night I called the hotel she was at because I found out from the record guys where she was. They put me through to her and I said, "Hello Sandi, this is Brian Wheat from Tesla."

She said, "Get the fuck outta here!" and told me about the ID sheet.

I'm like, "Oh wow, what a strange coincidence."

Then she said, "Why the fuck didn't you send me any of your records?" And I told her I lost the address, and I didn't have her phone number. I asked if I could have her number now. She said she had a boyfriend.

I said, "That's all right, I don't want to fuck you, I just want to call you and shoot the shit, man." So she gave me her phone number, and we started talking on the phone. Then she broke up with her boyfriend and we started dating. Finally, I talked her into seeing me on the road, and she became my girlfriend.

While we were in the studio recording, they were already talking about the next tour, either Poison or Cinderella. Both of them wanted us to go out with them. Everyone thought that Poison would do better business, so it wound up being them. We were out with them for five months during the first half of 1989. Back then I thought Bret Michaels was a punk. But we've toured with them since, and now we are good friends. We've all grown up since then. He just sent me some cologne, as a matter of fact. I had a lot of fun on that first tour. Chicks every night, getting fucked up. I always liked C.C. Deville. He wore his heart on his sleeve and didn't believe the hype. I think the other guys truly believed they were Led Zeppelin. C.C. was my favorite guy in that band.

Poison was a bit like David Lee Roth. But this time, when they tried to make us get out of the way when they were walking down the backstage hallway, we laughed at them. I remember Bobby Dall was walking down the hall with security, and they were yelling, "*Get outta da way*! Bobby Dall is comin'!"

I yelled back, "Fuck off! I ain't moving until Bobby Dall kisses my ass! Half the people here came to see Tesla, I ain't moving out of the way for nobody." As you can see, we had a little attitude by then, but it was all in fun. Some of us would get on the Poison bus and do massive amounts of blow, but I wasn't one of them. We went to the after-show parties and took their chicks, but it wasn't like Def Leppard. Onstage we were kicking their ass every night. But they were rock stars, and we were just musicians. Today, we are all pals, and I really love those guys.

We started that tour in the dead of winter. The first day I got off the bus to run, I fell right on my ass on an icy sidewalk. Fuck that. I didn't need a broken hip, so I had Dan buy me a Lifecycle that could be put in a road case. Back then, not a lot of hotels had exercise rooms. Now I'd just ride my ass off in the hotel room or our dressing room and watch TV while doing it. To this day it's a habit for me to exercise before a meal. It's like giving myself permission to eat.

For many years on tour I didn't eat breakfast and rarely a decent lunch either. Then we'd play, and I'd just pig out on dinner after the show. This was around eleven at night! After that, I'd just be sitting around the dressing room and bus until I went to bed. All those calories just turned to fat. I had to exercise that much harder to burn that off. Now I'll eat something like a normal breakfast when I get up around eleven, then some chicken and veggies in the afternoon around three. Then dinner became much less of a feast, just a time to replenish the calories burned during the show.

If I didn't have that discipline about eating, I could go sideways in a hurry on the road. From about six in the morning until eleven at night or so, there is always something to eat at a show. The catering company supplies whatever the bands and crews have specified in their contracts, some of it in the dining room, more in the dressing room, and even more on the buses. The bus could be the worst because you're trapped, rolling down the road to the next city with maybe four or five pizzas just calling your name. Taking a few tokes off a joint, a couple shots of scotch, or even just being bored can give you the munchies. Aside from all that, fans sometimes bring things for the band like cookies or a big box of chocolates. It's a constant test of willpower to stay on the plan. These days we're in more control of what we eat on the road. We'll have grilled chicken, fruit, and veggies instead of pizza. But as I said, nothing helps like getting results.

Cliff Burnstein was behind "Heaven's Trail" being the first single from *The Great Radio Controversy*. Jeff had the lyric, "I'm up on the stage, ready to kick ass," and Cliff wanted those to be the first words audiences heard from the new album. It did well, but it's not like it shot up the charts immediately. *Controversy* sold three hundred thousand copies and then started to stall, and people were saying, "Oh no, this could be the Sophomore Jinx." The second single was "Hang Tough," and it did nothing. Now we were worried. We noticed that the guys who came out from the record company while we were on tour with Poison would lie to us. We'd ask how the track was doing, and they'd say it was doing better than it was. Cliff told us what was happening. "Hang Tough" had stalled, and we were at the point where we're thinking, "Do we just give up and do another album, or do we take one more shot?"

So we said to Cliff, Tom, and Peter, "We want one more shot. We want to release 'Love Song' because we think it's a hit." We fought and pleaded with them. Tom went to David Geffen and persuaded him to let us put out another single. We shot a live concert video in Sacramento where we did an hour set and then two hours of playing "Love Song" over and over for the cameras. We put it out, and it started to make a bit of noise. People started playing it, but it took four months to develop. It was such a slow build, so gradual, so organic. George Cappellini, who does independent radio promotion for me now, was one of the radio guys at Geffen, and he said it was the longest-climbing single he had to work during his thirty years in the business.

We knew towards the end of the Poison tour that we were almost immediately going to do this so-called *Double Header Tour* with Great White. We switched off every night in terms of which band opened or closed the show. But we shared the lights and production. Each band had a few lighting specials that the other band didn't have, but mostly we shared the production. It was a smart tour to put together, and it gave both bands the opportunity to play in front of larger crowds than they otherwise would have. The tour ran until almost the end of 1989.

We started the *Double Header Tour* in Salem, Oregon, and Axl Rose's brother, Stuart Bailey, who wrote for *RIP Magazine*, was the valet for Great White. He had written a feature on Tesla, and we had gotten to be drinking buddies. When I arrived in Portland the night before the first show, we went out and got all fucked up. In one bar they refused to serve us. I offered to pay a hundred dollars for a shot, and they still refused. Stuart picked up a drink and threw it at the mirror in back of the bar (think Eddie Murphy in *48 Hrs.*) and it smashed. Glass went everywhere. The club security threw us both out on the sidewalk.

Back at the hotel I bumped into Great White's manager, Alan Niven, who also managed Guns N' Roses. I knew of Alan because he was one of the guys Tom originally wanted to manage Tesla, but we said no because we didn't like him. He said to me, "Don't worry if the record is not happening, you can be the support act," because "Hang Tough" had stalled. I remember calling up Joe Elliott drunk and crying and telling him what Alan said.

Joe said, "Tell the guy to fuck off and kick their ass every night!" Our audience was big enough to ensure the co-headline format because we had a big fan base, especially in places like Chicago and Detroit.

At a Shreveport, Louisiana, nightclub a few weeks later, things went much further. After downing some ungodly number of shots, Stuart and I decided to sit in with the band. Stuart was going to sing, I was gonna play guitar, Steve Whiteman, the singer from Kix, the opening act on that leg of the *Double Header Tour*, was gonna play drums, and Donnie Purnell, the bass player from Kix, was gonna play bass. Steve starts the drum intro to Led Zep's "Rock and Roll," and then I come in on Jimmy Page's monster guitar riff. Meanwhile Stuart is on one side of the stage all hunched over like a drunken Quasimodo waiting to ring his bell. He's screeching and screaming gibberish, and all of a sudden, he launches himself across the stage and crashes full speed into the keyboard rig, which fortunately nobody was playing at the moment. He went down in a heap, and the three keyboards and rack went tumbling off the stage onto the dance floor. The band grinds to a halt, and Steve and I are just looking at each other like, *What the fuck was that?* Things got kind of blurry after that. It was like a hallucination. Next thing I know, Dan McClendon grabs me and starts hustling me out of the club. The cops are called, and Stuart gets thrown in the back of a police car. He's not taking that very well, and he's screaming about kicking redneck cop ass and so forth. Dan managed to talk the cops out of arresting me along with him. Then one of the cops takes me aside and tells me that if I can't get Stuart to calm down, they're gonna take him down to the station, book him, and beat the crap out of him. I tried to get Stuart to back off, but he's out of his gourd, screaming about his constitutional rights, and I got nowhere. So off he goes in the squad car.

The next day he shows up at the gig looking like a human punching bag, all bruised and stitched up. He couldn't remember what they did, but based on his appearance, they were good at it. The cops said he fell in the shower. The happy ending is that Great White paid the poor keyboard player in the club band for damages and gave him a great story to tell his grandchildren.

At this point "Love Song" was moving along slowly. It started to do well on AOR (Album Oriented Rock) radio, but it wasn't a hit yet. Then it started selling. At this time, Peter and Cliff were with The Rolling Stones on their *Steel Wheels* Tour, and they have to be credited with the success of the song because—and this is the power of management and having a stable of artists—they went out and made deals with radio stations, saying, "If you put this Tesla song on your station and let the people vote on it, we'll give you a pair of Rolling Stones tickets to give away to the listeners." And this was with the CHR (Commercial Hit Radio) stations where Tesla wouldn't normally get played.

Ten weeks later the track went through the roof. We finished up the tour with Great White, and "Love Song" was in the top five on the Billboard Charts, and now we're really full of ourselves. At this point we've got a lot of money, some of the guys have bought houses, cars, boats, toys, all the shit. We weren't millionaires, but still it was more money than we'd ever seen. Lots of things happened to me during the next album, the band's third, but we'll get into that later.

Unplugged/Unhinged

Just before we started writing what was to be our third studio album, *Psychotic Supper*, Peter received a letter from Queenie Taylor, a woman in San Francisco who owned a nightclub with Boz Scaggs called Slim's. She was inviting us to play a full hour-and-a-half acoustic set. We had played one song acoustically, "Love Song," at the Bay Area Music Awards—BAMMIES—in San Francisco, and Queenie was there and really liked it. We told Peter that it's fine doing a couple of songs, but we're not playing a whole show acoustically. It's just something we didn't think about. It was a one-off, we had had fun, but that was it. We were an arena rock band. Who the hell wanted to think about a full acoustic set? He challenged us and said, "I bet that's because you can't." That's the brilliance of Peter in a nutshell. This fucking guy knew us inside and out. He knew how much pride we had and how much we loved a challenge. He played us perfectly. He's like a great coach, figuring out a way to make you step it up. That's just what he did. So we thought, *Fuck you!* and we put a ninety-minute kick-ass set together and played the club, doing two shows in one night.

The next day we were flying out because Mötley Crüe hired us to play six weeks of summer dates with them, mostly amphitheaters and a few stadiums. Mötley Crüe was touring in support of *Dr. Feelgood*, and they were pretty big. They were sober at the time and were really nice to us. They were certainly big rock stars, but they didn't act that way. Vince was a little weird at times, he wouldn't let anybody watch him during sound check, but they were cool and they liked Tesla a lot, even though Nikki had called us tomato farmers. It was almost like touring with Leppard. There were lots of women, and there was lots of partying. By this time, we were a bit more settled down. Jeff, Tommy, and Troy were married, I had just started dating my first wife, and Frank was going through a divorce.

That's when we really saw what it was like to have a hit single. Those crowds of twenty to thirty thousand people went bonkers when we played "Love Song." Peter and Cliff would pop out every week or two to see how things were going. During this time our fourth single was released, "The Way It Is." It made it to fifty-five in the Top 100 Singles chart. Although it did better than "Heaven's Trail" or "Hang Tough," it didn't equal or surpass "Love Song," so, in that sense, it was a disappointment.

There were a lot of off-dates on the tour, as Mötley Crüe would only play three days a week. We couldn't afford to take that time off, so we did a series of acoustic shows in Detroit, Boston, New York, and Philadelphia. We could do that now because of the Slim's shows. We had a whole set of original acoustic material and decided to add some covers. I picked the Beatles' "We Can Work It Out," Frank picked the Grateful Dead's "Truckin'," Skeoch chose "Mother's Little Helper" by the Rolling Stones, and Troy picked "Lodi" by Creedence Clearwater Revival. Jeff said he wanted to do the old '70s song "Signs." I knew of it because it was a hit by a band called the Five Man Electrical Band when I was a kid. One day on the tour, Jeff, Frank, and Tommy went to WAAF in Boston to perform it acoustically. Right away, the radio station got swamped with requests for that little three-piece version of "Signs."

We recorded and filmed the last show at the Trocadero in Philly. Unfortunately, the mobile truck didn't get a usable feed from the bass direct line. Dan McClendon was going to mix whatever we decided to do with it in Sacramento at Paradise Studios. We were thinking the recording would be just a toss-off, so we weren't going to spend a lot of money on it. We decided to overdub the bass there. I had one condition. Dan would roll the tape, and I would do it in one pass, beginning to end. This was like two or three in the afternoon. I had a couple of shots of scotch, sat down just like I did at the acoustic shows, and off we went. I didn't start any of the songs, so I had band cues for all of them. There were three breaks because a reel of tape only lasted about fifteen minutes. But if we didn't need to change tapes, I still would have done it in one fuckin' take.

After the Mötley Crüe tour we started writing songs for what was to be *Psychotic Supper*. One day our record company phones Cliff Burnstein to say that WAAF has been playing "Signs" in rotation, and it's in their top five most played songs! They said he should put us in the studio to record the song. We said that we had a whole acoustic show that we recorded and filmed in Philadelphia. They said, "Mix it up and maybe we'll put out an EP." So we mixed a few tracks, and they said, "This is really good. Mix the whole thing and we'll put it out as an album." That's how *Five Man Acoustic Jam* came about. The whole thing cost about thirty thousand dollars to make.

Frank and Troy didn't think it was good enough quality, cool enough, or whatever. Jeff and I thought it was a raunchy-sounding live record like Aerosmith's *Bootleg* album. Cliff and Peter loved it, especially Cliff. This was before all the *MTV Unplugged* hype. Not a lot of bands had the ability or balls to take their rock songs and play them acoustically. But we always loved the acoustic mini-set that

Led Zeppelin did in their shows, and we knew we were good enough to pull it off.

I thought we could sell about a hundred thousand copies, that it would be a cool underground thing. Much to everyone's surprise, "Signs" took off, went through the roof. It was all over MTV and the radio. It became the biggest record of our career, selling almost three million copies. It doesn't really bother me that "Signs," a song that we didn't write, was our biggest song, because it sounds like us. We could have written it, and a hit is a hit. We play it every night because the crowd loves it. Since we had filmed one of the shows, it seemed only natural to release a video of it as well. We'd never been the darlings of MTV, but "Signs" was the most requested video of 1991. And like the rest of the album, the video was just the one live take from the show, warts and all. Music industry insider and writer Bob Lefsetz, whose popular, informative, and entertaining newsletter is read by just about everybody in the biz, incredibly, said this: "From *Five Man Acoustical Jam*, the surprise hit, the inspiration for MTV 'Unplugged,' then again, so many claim that title. However, this is one of the most magical albums of all time. They say that *Live at Leeds* and *Get Yer Ya-Ya's Out* are the best live albums, I'd dispute that, *Five Man Acoustical Jam* is far superior."

The coolest thing about *Five Man* for me personally is that a few years later I was visiting Ross Halfin, and we went to a David Lee Roth show, which is where I first met Jimmy Page. Along with Paul McCartney and Freddie Mercury, he is a hero of mine. We were having a chat, and he says, "I really like your acoustic record."

I said, "What?"

He said, "*Five Man Acoustic Jam*, I love it."

I said, "Really? I didn't even think you would have known who I was."

He says, "Of course I know who you are. You're with Tesla, we're label mates." He was on Geffen when he did the *Outrider* record.

One of the greatest things that can happen is when one of your heroes tells you he likes your record. We hung out that night and had a good time. I wasn't sure if we would stay in touch but then, lo and behold, when the Robert Plant/Jimmy Page tour came through the Bay Area, Jimmy reached out and invited me to the shows. I went backstage to hang out and was surprised to find there was nobody back there but me. I was his private guest, and we just hung out talking about music. It was relaxed, laid-back, and really enjoyable. Our friendship just progressed from there.

Even though *Five Man Acoustical Jam* sounds fairly shitty, and it wasn't recorded on the best night, it gave us credibility and separated us from our contemporaries at the time. People thought, *These guys can really play. They're musicians*. I'm really proud of that record. It was the cheapest, easiest, and biggest record we ever made. It struck a raw nerve in people. It was an accident that gave us the time we needed to make *Psychotic Supper*, which had a lot of ups and downs; the madness was starting to set in.

7

The Abyss

The appropriately titled *Psychotic Supper* sessions were when the trouble started. Now we've got money, egos, drugs, wives, and everything's kind of built up out of proportion. Nothing in our lives prepared us for what was to come.

Five Man Acoustical Jam was flying off the racks, and now we'd started to see a lot of money. We've all got a few hundred thousand dollars in the bank, and it started to weigh on the band. Jeff started to get a bit nuts. He started doing a lot more drugs, got really skinny, and became more erratic. During the first two records he was fine. He would occasionally get fucked up, have a meltdown, and make comments like, "I don't want to do this anymore! It's ruining my life!" The next day he would apologize and say, "I didn't mean that, I was drunk."

Simultaneously, Troy decided that he's not going to come to rehearsals for pre-production. He wants to hang out with people he met in New York. They were a family, four brothers and three sisters. Troy would go over there and hang out with them, sing songs, and do a bunch of drugs. It was like one of those surreal scenes out of a

David Lynch movie. He told us he was going to record an album with this family. We said, "No, you're not, you're the fuckin' drummer in Tesla." It was Jeff who said, "Troy, you're fired. We'll get someone else." I don't think Troy thought the band would call his bluff.

We hired a Sacramento drummer, Mike Frowein, who came in, rehearsed with us, and we were fine with it. Then Troy came back after a week, crying and saying he was sorry, and he was back in the band. We made Dan tell Fro the news. That was kind of chickenshit of us. But we did buy him a whole new set of cymbals. That cost us a couple of grand.

That's how the writing process began on *Psychotic Supper*. Jeff was getting erratic, Troy was at the height of his addiction, and Frank and I were pretty productive. We had about thirty pieces of music ready, but Jeff wasn't doing any writing. He had just bought a house, was doing some remodeling and, I think, a lot of methamphetamine. Jeff will tell you that. He's pretty real. He'll also tell you that drugs fucked Tesla up.

I remember one time we had a band meeting with our business managers and accountants, and Jeff didn't show up. He sent his wife instead, who said, "I am me, and he is me, and we are Jeff." And we're like, *What the fuck?* He obviously wasn't in his right mind. The four of us were getting frustrated with that. Peter and Cliff wanted us to keep feeding the machine. We were riding high with a couple of platinum albums, but that was yesterday's news.

I took a break to get married in New Jersey. Sandi and I had this crazy wedding; it was huge. On one side there's my friends, about twenty people including Cliff Burnstein, Peter Mensch, Joe Elliott, Tom Zutaut, Lars Ulrich, and my family. On her side were about two hundred friends and relatives, some of whom came all the way over from Ecuador. We were married for about three and a half years. I got Cliff and Peter to manage her. She was a great girl, but we were very young.

It was around this time that I started having anxiety attacks. They were almost like out-of-body experiences. The technical term for them, I found out later on, was derealization/depersonalization episodes. I was getting stressed out from watching the first signs of instability in Tesla. I would look in the mirror, and I wouldn't feel like I was attached to my body. It was really fucking weird.

I came back from the wedding, and we carried on writing at a Sacramento rehearsal studio. If you look at band pictures from that time, like the inner gatefold of *Psychotic Supper*, you can see we have a worn look on us from three years of constant partying—all the drinking and drugging. Jeff was on an *RIP Magazine* cover. We were living the lifestyle and weren't taking care of ourselves.

Michael Barbiero and Steve Thompson came out, and we had half the songs written. Jeff was having problems finishing songs, and you can see on the album that there are co-writing credits with Michael Barbiero. He helped Jeff with the lyrics to the point of following him around with a pen and paper. Michael wound up writing lyrics for "Call It What You Want," "Song & Emotion," and "Edison's Medicine." That was when Jeff started unraveling. It started a downward spiral for him that hit bottom in Reno a few years later.

How the title of the album came about was from one night when Tommy, Frank, and I were eating, and there's no Troy, no Jeff. It was almost like we were having a therapy session at dinner, and Tommy said, "This is a psychotic supper." We were starting to unravel. Because once Jeff goes, the whole band starts falling apart.

I remember going to rehearsal one night and having a really bad anxiety attack. Steve Thompson took me outside, and I threw up. I didn't know what was going on. I thought I had a brain tumor or something. Steve took me to a hospital where his brother worked as a doctor, and he diagnosed me with the anxiety condition. He said I could take medication or therapy. I knew that I didn't want to get on a regimen of drugs. That's when I decided to go and see a psychiatrist.

Peter Mensch recommended his psychiatrist. His name was Isaac Herschkopf. At the time I thought psychiatry was bullshit. But Peter suggested I try it for a month and then decide. Isaac was a guy from New York who's treated a lot of famous people, including a baseball legend and many others. He was one of three psychiatrists who interviewed Mark Chapman after he killed John Lennon. I got on with him really well. He just tried to get me to a place where I was comfortable in my own skin. I didn't think I was that fucked up, but these anxiety attacks that I had were scary. Sure enough, after about a month, I did notice some easing of the attacks, so I continued to see him for the next ten years. I only stopped because after Tesla broke up, I couldn't afford to see him anymore. By that time, he had taught me how to manage things on my own.

The first panic attack I had was when I was fifteen. I remember it was Halloween, and I was riding my bike around the neighborhood, and I saw one of my older brother's friends. This guy, Larry Rau, was smoking a joint, and he said, "Hey man, do you want a hit on this?"

I said, "Sure, what is it?"

He said, "Panama Red." I guess I got good and high, because I started feeling like I was hallucinating. I started having this depersonalization. I found out later on that pot could bring on anxiety. When I went to school the next day, I had to go to the nurse's office because I didn't feel that well. My mom took me to the fire department because that's where you get your blood pressure checked, and it was high due to anxiety. But nobody knew about that stuff then. I figured out that the anxiety happened when I got stoned, so I stopped smoking marijuana. Alcohol didn't have the same affect, so I started drinking when I was fifteen. Later on I found out that a lot of my anxiety problems came down to me being an illegitimate child and seeing my mom go through a lot of pain at an early age. I wasn't mistreated, I always had food, and I wasn't sexually abused. My life to me was pretty normal. But it was a bit dysfunctional. There wasn't a strong family unit, even though certain members of my family would like to think that there was.

I'm a big advocate of psychiatry now. Isaac helped me out immensely. If you're honest and do what your therapist says, you can deal with a lot of issues in your life. I enjoyed spilling my guts. It made me feel better. Sometimes it was painful because I wasn't as honest as I could have been. But I was only lying to myself. He took me back to my childhood with the Freudian thing. We also did cognitive behavioral therapy. But the main thing with the doctor was my drinking—not how often but how much I drank.

TESLA WAS ON A ROLL. A lot of money was being spent; a lot of drugs were being consumed. There were wives on the road—Jeff's, Troy's, and mine. Frank was rollin' with the chicks. Some of the guys were taking drugs, and I was drinking and taking downers. Peter and Cliff were really involved, but you could tell that they were starting to get tired of our bullshit. We were at the height of our career at this time, so you weren't going to tell us much.

Steve Thompson managed to corral us all back together, and we finished writing the songs. When it came time to record *Psychotic Supper*, we refused to go back to Bearsville. We talked about recording in London, but that was too extravagant. We wanted to be where there was lots of energy. We wanted to be in Manhattan. I really dug the vibe in New York. It was so different than LA. Maybe the weather had something to do with it. It was gritty. Lots of people in a little space, no time to fuck around. Just get it done. That was the attitude I got. So we did the sessions at the Power Station. Aerosmith had recorded there back in the '70s, so that was good enough for us.

That decision turned out to be both a good and bad thing. Our managers probably thought it was going to lead to nothing but trouble. After all, we were young, successful, and out of control. And now were smack in the middle of New York City, 24/7. We had Michael Barbiero and Steve Thompson back as well. Jeff felt very comfortable with them, but the band wanted to go for something different. In the end Jeff got his way. That created a lot of animosity right off the bat between the producers and the band.

One difference from our previous albums was this time we each had our own apartment on the Upper West Side. They cost three grand apiece for the month: five apartments, one for each band member. That was $15,000 a month right there. Our stage manager/bass tech, Dan, shared my apartment. We needed a session roadie, so to speak, and Dan was our main guy on the road. There was nothing about what we liked and needed that he didn't know. Also, I had married Sandi by this time, and she had a house in New Jersey, so I spent most nights there. Only when I got too fucked up did I stay in Manhattan. So it was mostly Dan's room.

We had cocaine being brought to us and put on the recording budget. I wasn't into coke; the rest of the band was. I would drink. We'd record, then go to the China Club or the Limelight until eight the next morning and then come back into the studios. There was a time that Frank got too out of it, couldn't make it to a session, and Michael had to go to the apartment and sit with him. It was wild when we were partying. But we were laying down really good tracks. The recording process was simple; there was no drama. But then we were told, "OK, we'll mix this record at Bearsville," and that's when it got crazy.

Now, instead of being three of us, it was all five of us working on it along with Steve, Michael, Cliff, and Tom. You've got nine opinions, which was maybe justified on the first record because nobody knew what they were doing. The second record was maybe the best one, when there were a couple of us working on it and didn't have to go through a committee. None of us went to the mixes for *Five Man Acoustical Jam,* as half the band didn't even want to put that record out.

On the first two albums, we had only tracked at Bearsville, not mixed. They had a Solid State Logic board for mixing instead of a Neve. I think Neve consoles are like Cadillacs, classy and simple, but elegant. At the time, Solid State Logic consoles were real popular. It was the first board that had automation designed in, instead of added on like the Neves, so mixing was a lot easier and straightforward. Producers and engineers loved that. Mixing manually meant making every move on faders, EQ, effects, in real time. Make a mistake, and you'd have to start over. The problem with the SSL was that it just didn't sound as good as a Neve.

In the meantime, there was another bit of drama blowing up. After our first album, Guns N' Roses had gotten Steve and Michael to mix *Appetite for Destruction.* During the mixing of *Psychotic Supper,* they started work on *Use Your Illusion,* and they wanted Steve and Michael to work with them. I remember Slash calling me up and saying, "Dude, can you do me a favor and take a break and let Michael and Steve work with us?"

I said, "No! I mean I'd like to help you out, but the bottom line is that we're in the middle of making a record."

Michael and Steve wanted to stop and do the Guns record because it meant a lot of money for them. So they had resentments towards us because they lost that record, and to this day Michael Barbiero resents me for it. We've talked about it, and I said, "Michael, it took a year to mix *Use Your Illusion.* If you had done that, you would have lost the four other multiplatinum records you mixed. I didn't cost you any money." The bottom line is that he committed to doing Tesla, and I wasn't going to take a back seat to Guns N' Roses again.

We felt we had taken a back seat to them throughout our whole career. We were on the same label, and any time Guns N' Roses put out anything, they got the number one priority. Tesla would come in at four behind GNR, Aerosmith, and Whitesnake, even though we were responsible for the first successful rock record Geffen released. They put out *Done with Mirrors* by Aerosmith, and that was a flop. Guns N' Roses was eight months after us, and Barbiero/Thompson got the GNR gig because they'd produced *Mechanical Resonance*.

So here we are three years later. We've got Guns N' Roses wanting us to take a break. We've got Michael and Steve wanting us to take a break so they can make more money. Now there's friction between them and the band. The mixes at Bearsville aren't going well. Cliff and Peter want to bring in Terry Thomas. Jeff didn't want to let go of Steve and Michael. He's loyal, and once he starts something with someone, he wants to keep it going, which I understand, but the rest of the band wanted to try someone new.

The mixing sessions were fairly tense because of all the drugs and ego. We wound up recording in three different studios and mixing in three different studios. The mixes at Bearsville weren't cutting it, so we scrapped that and went to Right Track in New York City. That was another SSL board, and that sucked, so we scrapped those sessions. On top of that, when we heard the tracks of "What You Give" from the Power Station, they sounded awful, so we had to re-record the whole song.

We put our collective foot down and said that we needed to mix on a Neve, no matter how tough it was. So we ended up at the Hit Factory, where they had an old Neve. It was a ratty little studio. Aesthetically it was a dump. We started mixing the record for the third time and were finally getting mixes that we liked.

At the end of the day we wanted the best possible sound, to hell with how long it took. Mixing is often a long, hard process, not for someone who wants results in a hurry. Through the first studio changes, the entire band attended the mixing sessions. Then Jeff quit coming, then Troy stopped coming. After that, only Frank and I were at every session.

Tom Zutaut came in to listen to some of the tracks. We were working on "What You Give," and Tom asked Michael to increase the echo on the acoustic guitar. Michael didn't want to do it, but rather than argue with Tom, he used the old engineer's trick of turning a knob that didn't do anything at all. Most record company guys couldn't hear shit anyway, and usually the engineer would ask, "How's that? Better?" and the company dude would say, "Yeah...a little more. There, that's good." But Tom, who'd been around the block a few times, turned around and asked the assistant engineer, who worked for the Hit Factory, "Did he turn up the echo?"

The guy, knowing the legendary Tom Zutaut is putting him on the spot, threw Michael under the bus! "No, that knob doesn't do anything."

Tom turned back around and started yelling at Michael, "You worthless fuck! I'm sick of your bullshit! Don't be pulling that shit with me, I'll have your ass!" Frank and I just froze, whereupon Michael just stood up and walked out. Frank, Tom, and I wound up mixing six songs on the album by ourselves with the assistant engineer.

By then we didn't think we needed them, and they were getting tired of us. We couldn't see what Steve was doing. People close to the band were always complaining about how the guitars sounded, because it didn't sound like Guns N' Roses. Michael contributed a great deal to the album. He wrote half the lyrics. But we were all fucked up in a haze. There was just a lot of crazy shit going on.

Despite all the craziness, or maybe because of it, I think *Psychotic Supper* is the best record we ever made. Everything was right. We were nuts when we were making it, but the songs were the best-crafted songs we wrote, and the performances were the best we'd ever done. It's the best-sounding record, and it's got that Tesla spirit. Frank and I were stretching out with our individual writing styles, so the songs varied more than on the previous albums. And our personalities came through as well.

Everyone was expecting our first single to be a pop song, but we come out with the heaviest song of our career, "Edison's Medicine." We got an incredible amount of airplay on rock radio, but it kind of freaked everyone out. They were expecting us to ride the same horse we rode eight months earlier. We were pissed at everyone by then, after all the studio changes and fighting. I was starting to pay attention to how much money we were spending, which was a lot. And now we had to go on tour.

WE STARTED GOING TO EUROPE with our first record in 1987. There was a big buzz on Tesla because *Mechanical Resonance* had received a 5k rating in *Kerrang!*, which, at the time, was the rock bible in Europe. We went back there with Def Leppard on the *Hysteria* Tour, and that really exposed us to a bigger audience. It was time to get back there again.

While we were mixing *Psychotic Supper,* we went to a Scorpions show at the Meadowlands in New Jersey. Rudolf Schenker came up to me and said, "I love the acoustic record! I want Tesla to come and support the Scorpions in Europe." It was their biggest tour, as "Wind of Change" was a huge hit for them. The next day their manager, Doc McGhee, called Peter Mensch, and a few weeks later, off we went to Europe. But before starting that we decided to do one acoustic show in London at the Astoria, and it was a fuckin' killer. Thanks to some smart promotion, we even played an acoustic show for the king of Sweden in his private palace, all fucked up on his booze. We had a great time.

At that point, Troy had finally gotten sober. He got into a treatment program before we went on tour, and we didn't know about it. Just before we set off, he comes to us and says, "Guys, can you do me a favor?"

We say, "Sure, what's up, Troy?"

He says, "I got clean and sober, could you not do drugs and drink around me? I don't care if you do them, but could you not put it in my face?" To be honest, no one really respected him on that request. Guys were doing blow and smoking pot on the bus. I felt like we let him down. I didn't smoke pot or do blow, I only drank, so I thought I was all right. When I went out, I never went out with him, I always went with the crew guys because they were crazy. I admire Troy because he stayed sober through it all, and it wasn't like he got a lot of help from us. We were like, "Yeah, whatever. It's your problem."

During the tour in Germany, some guy broke into Troy's room, put a gun to his chest, and said, "Give me your money." Troy managed to calm the situation and get the guy out of his room without giving him anything. When we heard the story, we thought Troy was high or hallucinating, but I believe it did happen.

We came back to the UK, and our first gig was at the Hammersmith Odeon, now known as the Carling Apollo. It was sold out, there was a big buzz around the band, and the press was all over us. This was the show that could have established the band in the UK and Europe. I can't tell you what happened, but the set wasn't put together very well. We were being self-indulgent. We played a bunch of songs off the new album first, and they just never got into that frenzy. The crowd was flat, and we feed off the crowd, so we got kind of flat.

It was a seated venue and, with Tesla, it's always better if the audience is standing, because they are rowdier and more into it. We started the show, and the vibe from Hammersmith wasn't how we remembered it when we played with Def Leppard three years earlier. The crowd was subdued, and the energy wasn't happening.

Frank sat down Indian style in the middle of the set facing Troy, because the crowd was lame. I don't think the band was aware of the magnitude of that gig. No matter if the audience is shit, you've still gotta throw out all the energy you've got. The show was terrible.

Mensch came backstage and said, "You've just fucked your career in Europe." Our agent, John Jackson, just had this ghostly look on his face.

The next morning, Ross Halfin called me and said, "You were shit, you need to change your set. You need to open with 'Cumin' Atcha Live.' You can't play so many new songs that nobody knows." We had eight shows left in the UK, so we rearranged the set, and the remaining shows were great. But for some reason, from this one show, the press deemed us self-indulgent and boring. It killed any momentum we had built up in Europe during our previous visits.

Peter and Cliff didn't want us to go back to Europe after that trip because they didn't believe we could make money there. What could we do except come back sixteen years later and play an amazing gig at the Shepherd's Bush in 2006? It was probably the best gig we ever did in the UK. Now every time we go back to Europe, we play great, and the reviews are good. We've sold out a lot of the shows on our own and went three years in a row. Some fans had been waiting since 1987 to see us. But it definitely wasn't as big as it was in America.

When we got back to America, we did our first and only headlining tour of arenas and amphitheaters. The whole thing lasted about twelve months. Jeff got better on the road. He got healthy and stopped being erratic like he had been in the studio. Maybe it was because he wasn't around the people who were supplying him with drugs. He did have a couple of meltdowns where he said he wanted to quit the band, but those passed quickly. Still, I always felt on that album and tour that the rug could be pulled from under my feet at any moment. I never felt secure in the band after *Psychotic Supper*, even though we were at the height of our career with our last-ever platinum album. It was all elevating my stress level.

So now we were legitimate headliners. On the Poison tour we had hired Howard Ungerleider to be our road manager and lighting director. He had been with Rush forever. Now that we were touring as top dogs, he was able to get us really nice hotel rooms at the Ritz-Carlton and the Four Seasons and so forth.

The whole show production was now under our control as well, but as a band we were pretty much hands off. We had a great lighting director and sound engineer, and we let them design the light rig and the PA. We didn't really pay attention to what that cost. We didn't get ripped off or anything, we just didn't get involved.

We released five singles and made five videos for that record. It was the pinnacle of our career. The tour was successful; we made a lot of money. We were known, it was a good time, but it was also a bad time because you could see that things were starting to fall apart. We weren't hanging out together like the early days. We were doing two-hour-and-fifteen-minute sets, which put a real strain on Jeff's voice. That was insane. We should have never put that on him. We weren't thinking about what we were doing to him, and he didn't want to let anybody down, so he was trying his hardest.

There was an incident in Battle Creek, Michigan, at the first show on the tour. Peter Mensch came out to see us and was going to spend a week with the band, hang out, and critique the show. The acoustics were terrible in the arena, and the band wasn't in a great mood afterwards. We got into this discussion in the dressing room, and all of a sudden Jeff starts having a go at Peter. He gets into this kind of manic state of mind and yells that he doesn't give a fuck about hit records, and it escalated from there into a huge argument. Peter said, "You guys are fuckin' nuts," and left. We were shooting a video on tour, and that's all on tape.

Another time Cliff came to Shreveport, Louisiana, to have a band meeting, and same thing; Jeff started having a go. Cliff just looked at us and said, "You guys are unmanageable," and left. I think management was thinking, "This is becoming a lot more work than it should have to be."

After the *Psychotic Supper* tour, we came home and told Cliff and Peter that we needed some time off, and they were cool with that. We'd been doing this for six years, and we needed a break. It was 1992.

The Party's Over
a.k.a. Pills, Thrills, and
Backstage Fistfights

Peter called one day early in 1993 and said that Hollywood producers putting together the new Arnold Schwarzenegger movie, *Last Action Hero*, wanted us to record a song for it. So Tommy, Frank, and I got together and wrote a song at Tommy's house. Then we went to Troy's to record a demo, and Jeff finished the lyrics. The record company accepted the demo and gave us $100,000 dollars to record it, an incredible amount of money. We went to the Record Plant in Sausalito to record, and someone in the band was not at his best. When we listened back, we decided certain parts were unusable, so the entire session was scrapped. We moved over to Skywalker Ranch, which is George Lucas's place where he does Star Wars. It's a crazy expensive studio that costs about $5,000 dollars a day. We spent $100,000 dollars recording just one song, and it was horrible! We tried mixing it a few times with different people and didn't like it. We thought we had the title track of the movie, and it ended up being played at the end when the credits were rolling—which I guess was appropriate because *Last Action Hero* was the least successful movie that Arnold made.

IT WAS A DIFFICULT TIME; a black cloud was forming over the band. Right when we should have been focused on making the best record of our career, our *Back in Black*, we chose to get fucked up. It was also at this time that our contract was up with Geffen. We went to them and said we wanted to test the seven-year law. In California you can only be signed to a contract for a maximum of seven years. It goes back to the days when director Hal Roach had those kids in *The Little Rascals* signed up for the rest of their lives. So we said we wanted $12 million to sign a new contract, or we would test the law. David Geffen said to Peter and Cliff, "Why are they doing this, are they going to break up?"

They said, "Of course not! The band's great, they've made four platinum records, why would they break up?" Even though I knew we were on our last legs, Geffen coughed up $5 million (it was a "hybrid" arrangement; part of it was from the old contract and part of it was toward the new).

We were rollin', man. We were rich! Instead of getting back in the studio, we started spending money. I don't think we saw each other for eight months. I had married Sandi, so I had one house in Sacramento and one in New Jersey. She was home when I was on tour, and I was home when she was on tour. The first time we were off the road together was during the writing of *Bust a Nut*. I came to find out that she didn't care for Sacramento all that much, and I didn't like New Jersey, so even when we were together, one or the other of us wasn't that happy with where we were. On top of that, her career, unfortunately, wasn't really going anywhere. I'd asked Peter and Cliff to help her out, but nothing came of that. That was frustrating for Sandi. She is a great talent, but she may have been better off being more of a pop singer than fronting a hard rock band. When we got along, we were good pals, but when we fought, we fought hard. I'm Italian and she's Ecuadorian, so there is some fuel there. I never hit her or touched her in anger, but I did take out my frustrations on the furniture and walls with a baseball bat. We were both very stubborn, and it was hard for either of us to compromise. At the end of the day she wanted a big family, and I didn't want to have kids. Since I never really had a father, I didn't know how to be one, and I didn't want to experiment on some kid.

When we started work on *Bust a Nut*, we decided to bring producer Terry Thomas over from England. We worked on one song with him, "Action Talks," and agreed he was the man to use for the album. We got more songs written and went into preproduction. We first heard about Terry through Joe Elliott, who told us about his work with Bad Company. Then we found out that he played in a band called Charlie. It's a tremendous asset when a producer is a musician. Terry put together some great sounding demos; we really liked him a lot.

Bust a Nut was recorded at Fantasy Studios in Berkeley, across the bay from San Francisco. It is the studio where Creedence Clearwater Revival recorded all their classic albums. I made a conscious decision to not repeat the mistakes of the last album, the first of which was going to the East Coast when we could easily do it on the West Coast. We wanted to be close to home, and that's why we chose Fantasy. Looking back, it may have been a bad decision. Maybe it would have been better if we had been away where there wouldn't have been so many distractions.

It was what it was, but there were fun moments making that record. Unfortunately, the album was a little disjointed. You can kind of tell that we were falling apart, unraveling. But there are a handful of songs on that album that still hold water today. I think the proof of the pudding is in the live set, things I still want to showcase to audiences. For me, they are "Try So Hard," "Wonderful World," and "Mama's Fool." There was some stuff that wasn't so good, like "The Gate/Invited." I look at that today and think, *God, what was I thinking?* I thought I was writing this "Band on the Run" song, but it wasn't. "Need Your Lovin'" was a single, but I didn't care for that song; I thought it was trite. I liked "Earthmover." It had a twisted, fucked-up bridge that was really cool. "Solution," I didn't like that. "She Want She Want" I like now. That song is like "Be a Man" for me. I didn't like it then, but I like it now. "Action Talks" goes in the same category as "Rock Me." "Cry" was cool; it was one of my songs, but it wasn't an A song, it was a B song. "A Lot to Lose," great song. That was me, Frank, and Jeff. That's a classic. "Rubberband," which I like, is another one I wrote, but it never really lived up to its potential.

The sessions were mostly good. Jeff was either into it or out of it, depending on what he was doing. I remember him coming in and sleeping all day. It was a really hard record to get done because we were coming from different directions. Terry Thomas should have gotten a medal for that album. He put it all together and got us all in one place to finish it. Terry would tell Jeff, "Let's start at one o'clock," and Jeff would show up at nine o'clock at night. It was the first record where I split after I had done my parts. Troy was sober, so he was like, "You guys are out of your minds." I was doing my usual bottle of scotch a day. Frank was just being the usual Frank. He always dabbled in alcohol, blow, or weed.

Peter and Cliff's attitude to me was, "You deal with it." They'd had it. Cliff didn't like a lot of the songs we'd submitted, and we were like, "Fuck it, we're making this record, and there's nothing you can do about it."

Terry wanted to mix the album in England. I have always had a thing for England, so Frank and I went over and mixed at Mayflower Studios in London. We were going to be there for five weeks, so I asked Sandi to come with me. She didn't want to, and it was at that time that our marriage started falling apart.

Sandi wanted to have five kids, which is exactly what she has now. The funny thing is that she did exactly what she wanted to do, and I've done exactly what I wanted, which is not have kids. Don't ever marry someone who has the same job as you. It never works out. We were crazy in love, but we were young and trying to figure it out. But we didn't connect in some areas. And that whole thing about living with someone before marrying them is absolutely true, because once we started living together, we started having problems.

It was a short marriage. Hindsight being twenty-twenty, I could have been cooler to her. She could have been cooler to me. Sandi also got way into religion and I didn't, which caused a rift. So, fundamentally we had differences, but again, we were just young. We got into this marriage because we were in love. But just being in love sometimes isn't enough.

Thankfully today, we have a great relationship. She married a great guy and has five beautiful kids. We're all good friends now. Even our spouses are good friends, and I love her kids and husband. They are like my family. So sometimes, as the Rolling Stones said, you can't always get what you want, but you get what you need.

At this time, I was getting frustrated by everything. We thought we had created the next *Back in Black* and were convinced that we were poised for even greater success. Unfortunately, it was a couple of years too late, because the grunge thing had kicked in. We didn't realize that. In our world, we were still at the top of our game. We were used to being the champions of AOR radio for almost ten years, and all of a sudden with the album we think is our massive breakthrough record, the radio stations aren't down with us because we're not grunge, we're a "hair band" or "butt rock." *Bust a Nut* did OK. We got a gold record out of it.

One cool thing that happened in the middle of *Bust a Nut* was that Atlantic Records approached us to record a song for a Led Zeppelin tribute album, *Encomium*. They paid us some crazy amount of money, and we went in and cut a version of "The Ocean." While we were doing that, Peter and Cliff came to us and said, "We've got this song we want you to record because we think it will be a big hit like 'Signs.'" It was called, "Games People Play," written by Joe South, and had been a hit in the '70s. I fuckin' hated the song, and I still hate it. Frank and I were like, "Fuck that! This is bullshit." We could see right there that the record company didn't think that we had a hit record. Neither did Peter or Cliff.

We recorded "The Ocean," and we absolutely slammed that. We're huge Zeppelin fans. Then we did "Games," and I remember I had to do my bass part three times because I was so pissed off that I was playing too hard. Terry was like, "If you don't play it right, I'm going to play it for you!"

"The Ocean" came out on the Japanese release of *Bust a Nut,* but it didn't make the Zeppelin tribute. Robert Plant said he wanted the album to feature all the alternative bands of that time, so we got nixed. I was really disappointed, especially since Ross played the track to Jimmy Page, and he really liked it.

It was a mad time. Everyone was out of their fuckin' minds. Management wasn't into the record we were making, the record company wasn't into the record we were making, and they had just given us $5 million. Our A&R guy, Tom Zutaut, was nowhere to be found. He didn't show up until we were mixing in London. The band was unraveling, and I was just trying to keep it all together. After we finished the album I went home, filed for a divorce, and moved to midtown Sacramento.

We went on tour to promote *Bust a Nut* and, initially, it looked like it was going to be a big record. We had loads of airplay on the first single, "Mama's Fool," but grunge, again, had just kicked in, and we weren't aware of it. We were kind of oblivious to what was going on around us because we were only really concerned with what we were doing. We weren't interested in what other people were doing or what the scene was. Looking back, we had unrealistic expectations for that album. We knew what we needed to do, we just didn't do it. We were too indulgent and not critical enough. Our standards should have been higher. We expected to be back headlining arenas, but it was mostly three- to five-thousand-seat theaters. Some fans say it is their favorite album, and it has some strong songs, but it's inconsistent.

Grunge didn't kill Tesla, but the perception was that we had four platinum records and then *Bust a Nut* "only" went gold. The word was Tesla was on the way out. That was not even close to the truth. We could have easily carried on making gold records. It was the internal shit that did it.

In Detroit, where we were starting the tour, Tommy suddenly had to leave due to some personal issues. The tour manager took him to the airport and sent him home. We played as a four-piece for the first leg of the tour, about three months. It was difficult at times because every song we had was written for two guitars. Other times, it was kind of fun to play with only the one guitar. Frank got to really stretch out, and I had more room to try some stuff that I normally wouldn't have, a fill here and there, getting more treble with my tone.

Tommy went into rehab and everyone phoned him, but I refused. Cliff Burnstein said, "You need to phone him," and I said, "I don't want to, I've got nothing to say to him. In my opinion, he's a fuckup." In the end Cliff persuaded me to call, saying it would be good for the both of us. Tommy rejoined the tour when we were supporting Lynyrd Skynyrd, and the first couple of shows were great. Everyone was happy to see him. He was sober, or soberish. It was the Tommy we knew and loved. Two weeks later he was back to his old tricks. We were in Buffalo, New York, and we started "Song & Emotion," which is just Tommy and Frank during the intro and first verse, very quiet arpeggios. There's about fifteen thousand people in the audience. When it was time for him to join the song, Skeoch blows his part, and the whole crowd goes, *Awwwwwwwww!*, like a big sigh. We finish the set, go down to the dressing room, and Jeff confronts Tommy. Skeoch makes a lame excuse and, amazingly, says, "Yeah, fuck it, Jeff, let's just quit the band."

Then Troy has an argument with Jeff about being clean and sober and the Twelve-Step Program. Jeff tells Troy to fuck the Twelve-Step Program and *wham!* Jeff and Troy get into a big fistfight. Frank and I are sitting on a couch eating ice cream cones off the table in front of us, and these two fuckers are beating the fuck out of each other. In the old days we would have broken it up. But we thought, *Fuck it! Let them just beat each other's asses.* We just sat there and watched it like it was a boxing match on TV.

We've had a few brawls over the years. The first time we went to England, Jeff and Troy got into a fight in front of Peter Mensch. It was the first time we had hung with Peter. We were playing in Sheffield, and Troy had started "Cumin' Atcha Live" really slow. After the show Jeff commented on it, and Troy says, "Well I'm the fuckin' drummer and I'll set the tempo any fuckin' place I want!"

And Jeff says, "No you won't!" and they start fighting in the dressing room.

Peter tried breaking them up, screaming, "You fuckin' guys are worse than the Young brothers!" I guess Malcolm and Angus used to duke it out a lot. Jeff and Troy were like Ali vs. Frazier, rematch after rematch, Thrilla in Manila.

I've had a fight with Jeff. We were both drunk on whisky, and I accused him of doing blow. He denied it. Actually, I don't think he was stoned, I was just really fucked up at the time. I feel bad about that because Jeff is one of my favorite guys on the planet.

No one has ever gotten into a brawl with Frank. I think he would kick everyone's ass. He's studied karate and martial arts. I wouldn't want to tangle with him. He's a big guy, too, with strong hands. I don't know if he's got that crazy temper like me, Jeff, and Troy. We have short fuses; we can just go off. Frank is mellow. But arguing and fighting has always been the Tesla way. Today we just like to call them "discussions."

Tommy was asked to leave again, and this time it was for good, or so we thought. I'll be honest, I was not sorry to see him go. He just wasn't a nice guy. I was tired of him being the loudest guy in the room when he got fucked up. Everyone was taking the brunt of his shit. We finished the Skynyrd tour without him and went home.

Jeff missed Tommy the most. When Tommy left, it was hard on him. Frank, Troy, and I were quite vocal about not missing him, and I think that caused a rift between us and Jeff. We gave Tommy more chances than he deserved. When we re-formed in 2000 we brought him back, but the same thing happened. He was just out of control.

Tommy always blamed me for him getting kicked out. I'd say, "God damn it, Tommy, I didn't fire you. I'm just one guy. Three other guys voted unanimously, but you always took your shot at me!" I was the messenger. I was the guy who would say, "Hey look, you're fucking up." Everyone else would say it but then not back it up. It still happens to this day. I got in a huge argument with Jeff the other day in the dressing room.

Everyone came to me, the manager, the tour manager, the band, saying, "You have to talk to Jeff, we have to talk to Jeff." We sit at this fuckin' round table, and I'm the predominant one, no one else says anything, and I'm thinking, *Well, this is fucked up. Me and Jeff never argue*. Depending on the day of the week, he's maybe my favorite guy.

I've said a lot of things about Skeoch. Some out of spite, some out of sadness. But when you get down to it, when he was on, he had an incredible work ethic. He always wanted to work; he always wanted to do well. At some point though, the drugs got hold of him. He lost his focus and his drive, and he wasn't a nice guy when he was like that. He did some shit, and said some shit, that left permanent damage on people, especially me. But I hold no ill will against him.

I could see the band was coming apart. I'm not a big fan of southern rock, so the Skynyrd tour wasn't all that enjoyable for me. I do like the Allman Brothers, but that's about all. There was a lot of coke on that tour, but I wasn't doing any of it. I discovered coke a year later on the *Time's Makin' Changes* Tour, just when my buddy Frank stopped doing it!

All of this crap that was coming down, my marriage ending, the band falling apart, the drugs and drinking, caused my autoimmune disease to flare up for the first time since I was thirteen. I had a severe bout of colitis, which caused my intestines to get inflamed. I was shitting blood and was in severe pain. I wasn't taking very good care of myself, as I was going through a self-destructive phase. I was still running six miles every day, but after the sun went down, I'd get a couple of grams of coke and a bottle of scotch and party until the sun came back up. Then do it all over again. I was having a good time...I thought. In reality it was the beginning of a long downward spiral.

WHEN I WAS STILL LIVING OUT IN THE SACRAMENTO SUBURBS, my friend Darin Wood, the singer from 58 Fury, was living downtown. I'd go see him occasionally and hang out, and I realized I really dug the downtown energy and all the things to do. Sandi didn't want to live downtown because she thought it wasn't safe there. So when we divorced, I moved into a little bungalow downtown with my nephew Butch. The owners didn't want to rent to me, a long-haired freaky type. They said, "We don't want you working on your Harley in the front yard."

I said, "I don't have a Harley, but I'll pay you six months' rent in advance...in cash." That got their attention. I stayed there while the divorce was getting done. I was drugging pretty good by then and was listening to a lot of funk. Kool & the Gang was on my turntable constantly; sometimes I'd just play "Jungle Boogie" over and over. You do that kind of shit when you're high.

I knew I wanted to live downtown and had always liked the old Victorian houses. There was one across the street from the Oasis Ballroom, and I used to tell myself I was going to have a pad like that. So I went shopping for a Victorian. I found one in this little hilltop area downtown called Poverty Ridge. It was called that because in the old days, downtown used to flood, and the poor folks would come up there and hang out until the water receded. This place was big, had a pool. I put in a bid, but someone outbid me.

I had a real estate agent who was showing me available places. He was cool, but he had a really bad toupee. I'd never really been close to a guy with one before. It just fascinated me that someone would wear a thing like that. I was smoking a lot of weed at that time, so I'd just stare at him; it tripped me out, that rug.

One early evening on a break from the Skynyrd tour we were driving down J Street to his office, and I see a Victorian with a For Sale By Owner sign out front. It wasn't even listed. I said "Stop, stop!"

He said, "You don't want that, it's zoned commercial."

I told him, "I don't care," and I walked up the steps and rang the doorbell. This old guy answered the door. I said, "You're selling this? Can I see it?"

He said, "Sure, come on in." I'm standing in the foyer, and the first thing I saw was a beautiful staircase going upstairs, and the wall was covered in stamped leather, original stuff. The parlor was right in the front, and the living room, dining room, and kitchen were off to the back.

The next day I made him an offer. He wanted $285,000, and I offered $280,000, and that was it, sold. The guy, whose name was James, lived there for another four months downstairs while I started remodeling the upstairs. When he moved out, I started redoing the downstairs. I resurfaced all the wood flooring, patched and painted the interior. The outside was a kind of battleship gray. I didn't get to that for a couple of years, but when I did, I went all-out on the color scheme. I got an award from the city for the exterior paint job.

Butch and I moved into the Victorian. I had my grand piano, my bed, a dining room table, and that was it. Some lawn furniture was in the parlor! So later when I went out on the *Time's Makin' Changes* tour, and even part of the Lynyrd Skynyrd tour before that, I started going to antique shops and buying shit. I just left it all in the stores then sent one of our roadies out in a U-Haul truck across the country to pick up everything and bring it back. I bought antiques because I had a house built in 1895. The house drove it; you wouldn't put that stuff in a contemporary house. That's why I have a lot of antiques. I didn't have any of that stuff before. Now I had a place to send them to.

The artwork will appreciate, hopefully. I collect Chiparus statues. They're fashioned from bronze and ivory. I don't really think of them in terms of, "Well, if I buy this, in ten years it's going to be worth that." They're beautiful, and I would see one and I would dream that someday I'd be able to have one in my house. I first saw a Chiparus statue on the cover of the Wings' greatest hits album. When I bought my house, I started collecting books and discovered that I like Art Deco. I started doing research, and there was all this Chiparus stuff that came up. I thought, "That was the thing that was on Wings' greatest hits, that's it." Demétre Chiparus was the king of bronze and ivory and marble statues in the Deco period. Then there was Louis Icart. I collect Eckhardt stuff too. I like to collect jukeboxes. I have three jukeboxes: a Wurlitzer from the '30s, a Seeburg from the '50s, and a Rock-Ola from the '40s. I collect old Victrolas and Coke machines. I like nostalgia; I like to have things when I think they were, like, pure. Most of my music collection is from the '70s because I felt the '70s were the purest era for music, even more so than the '60s. The greatest music in all genres was from the '70s.

I like art and antiques. I'm not a collector of vehicles. I own two Minis, very simple. I have a nice Indian motorcycle, and I've got a Royal Enfield with a sidecar that Steve Emler, our soundman, built me. I used to have a Kawasaki that looked like an Indian, which is why I got the Indian. I wanted a real one, and it's always handy to have a spare bike around. I'm not really a motorcycle guy, but I like my Indian. Riding a motorcycle clears my head.

I collect vinyl records. When I was a kid we had vinyl records. When CDs came along, Tesla was a signed act, and I was on the road a lot. You could pack a road case drawer full of CDs, and they wouldn't get all fucked up like records would. You could skip tracks; you didn't need a record player. There were lots of reasons I started buying CDs, but mostly it was convenience. I wasn't too critical about the sound difference back then.

In 2012 I started hanging out with Jimmy Page and Ross Halfin quite a lot. We'd be walking around London, and they'd want to duck into a record shop, because by then vinyl was becoming popular again. I wasn't interested, so I'd see a bookstore and go there instead. Later we'd be eating at a pub or something, and they'd break out these records they'd bought. Jimmy would say, "Brian, the records are so much better sounding than CDs."

I'd say, "I don't know, man."

He said, "Trust me Brian, vinyl kicks CD's ass."

One night, Monique and Jimmy and I were going out to dinner in London for his seventieth birthday. I was giving him one of my

Hofner basses as a present. We were meeting at his place. Before we left to eat at the Troubadour, he said, "Check out this record." He puts on an old 1956 version of "Train Kept A-Rollin'" by the Johnny Burnette Trio. It just fuckin' blew my mind. It sounded fantastic. There was a warmth to it that CDs just don't capture. And Jimmy didn't have some crazy big-ass stereo. It was fairly normal, maybe a McIntosh amp, no big deal. I thought to myself, *He's fuckin' right*. After that I went on a vinyl-buying frenzy. I think I have about five thousand albums on vinyl now. Being friends with Jimmy Page is one of my favorite things in life. And not just because I was such a Zeppelin freak growing up. Honestly, it has nothing to do with that. I mean of course, it's cool to think that that is the guy I had up on my wall. But we never talk about Led Zeppelin. Jimmy is just a smart, thoughtful, artistic soul who is fun to hang out with. He's very generous and is great company. Cultured and elegant, he definitely has a charisma that is different than anybody else I know. But at the end of the day, wherever we happen to be, from exotic places in Thailand or London or at my house in Sacramento, at the end of the day he's my friend. And I respect that friendship immensely.

FOR YEARS BEFORE I BOUGHT THE J STREET HOUSE, I didn't think about where I was living, I didn't think I was throwing away my money. I knew the best investment you could make was in real estate. Cliff Burnstein told me that when we got that contract money from Geffen. But I didn't immediately. I just wanted an old Victorian house, and I thought, *Well, buy a house versus renting it, you're throwing your money away*. So I bought the house. But that's not the same house that I bought. I put a lot of sweat equity into it and improvements. I took a second mortgage when Tesla broke up, and I had five years of no touring income. I toured with my other band, Soulmotor (which you'll read about later), but I didn't make any money. No real income except for whatever my royalties were, which were unrecouped because Geffen had just given me an advance. Basically it was my publishing royalties.

I did take some home equity cash out of the house, which is why today I still have a mortgage. But I also built the back studio on it. At first I didn't have the time or patience to build a proper studio, so I just converted a bedroom upstairs to a control room and had a small recording space in an adjacent room. I had that rig until 2003. It was primitive for sure. When I got remarried, my wife would be sleeping in our bedroom across the hall, and I'd be recording guitars at four in the morning. She had a job then and had to get up at 7:00 a.m. She was a real trooper about that.

Last Blast of the Century/
The Birth of the Slugger

With Tommy gone there were just the four of us, and Geffen Records decided that they wanted to do a greatest hits album, which is always a sign of, "Goodbye, it's been nice having you on our label."

They asked us to write two new songs for the compilation and gave us around a quarter-of-a-million-dollar budget. We tried to put some new material together, and it wasn't happening. So Terry Thomas came out and put one song together with Jeff called "Steppin' Over." But we couldn't put together a second song because the band was fried, and people were fucked up. I think everyone realized the end was upon us. Then I became a drug addict.

Time's Makin' Changes came out, and we went on the road as a four-piece. Jeff was pretty fucked up. He wasn't taking care of himself, and his voice sounded like it was shredded from the drugs. I was looking for a little less reality, and by the time we started the tour, I discovered Ecstasy.

The first time I took Ecstasy was when I went to England with my brother Buddy. It was after my divorce from Sandi, and I was visiting a girlfriend. Buddy had met a girl there too. One night we went out drinking at a club called the Borderline, and Buddy's girlfriend came up to me and said, "Here, take this," and popped an Ecstasy tablet in my mouth.

Buddy was already high and said, "Don't worry, man, I'll take care of you." I was terrified. I had never taken a hallucinogenic in my life. All I'd ever done was drink alcohol and take downers.

All of a sudden this thing came on me, and I'm like, *"Whoaaahh."* I had to sit down because I started to freak out. My brother got some water for me, and he was like, "Just go with it, dude, it's like mescaline. It's going to be beautiful, man!"

All of a sudden it felt like someone had thrown a warm blanket over me, and everything was beautiful, and I'm like, "Man, this is fucking amazing! If everyone took this, we wouldn't have any more wars." I was fucked up! We spent the night at the Borderline dancing and drinking orange juice. Then I went back to my chick's house and fucked the shit out of her for eight hours. That night I fell in love with Ecstasy!

Between the *Bust a Nut* and *Time's Makin' Changes* tours, I hung out at a club near my house that was owned by a friend of mine, a crazy character I'll call "Cocaine Keith." Anyway, I'm in the back office at the club, and he asks, "Do you want to smoke some grass?"

I said, "Yeah, cool!" Then all of a sudden he started chopping out some blow and asked me if I wanted a line. And I'm like, "No I don't do it, it's not my thing." And then I thought, *What the fuck, I'll do some to be sociable.* I knew the band was breaking up, so that's how I dealt with my depression. Part of my thinking was if this is what's fucked the band up, then I want to see what it's all about. So I did this line, and all of a sudden I get this same euphoric high that I got on Ecstasy. I'm like, *I really like this, this is really cool.*

So, I call up the band's dealer, who got the coke for everyone in Tesla except for me. He used to keep away from me because he knew I didn't like it. I said, "Hey man, can you bring me an eight ball?"

He's shocked and asks, "What? For who?"

I said, "For me."

He said, "Man, you don't do that shit."

I snapped, "Well I do now so bring me a fuckin' eight ball!" I sat in my room and did the whole lot in one evening listening to music with a disco ball spinning above my head. That is when I started running around with this guy Vito, a metal artist who made some stuff up for me. He was a dark character. He had this crazy haircut, and all the chicks liked him. He was a cool dude. He actually grew up a couple of blocks away from me when I was a kid. We hung out, did drugs, fucked chicks. We'd get chicks into my house, get them naked and paint them with acrylic paint. We were getting kind of freaky!

One night I did eight hits of Ecstasy and Vito finally said, "Hey, Brian, I don't think we can get any higher, we should probably stop." Thinking about it now, I might have been trying to kill myself, or at least didn't care if I did.

I had this hooker girlfriend, Lucy, I had met at a local music joint. We always used to flirt but one night I went up to her and said, "Hey, do you want to be my fuck buddy?" The next thing you know, we're upstairs in my house getting high. She had an incredible Soma habit. Soma is a muscle relaxant and makes you almost comatose. Now there were all these people doing blow and Ecstasy downstairs while I'm fucking Lucy upstairs. She was into being knocked around and I'm like, *This isn't cool, I'm not into this shit!*

But the more coke I did, the more I was into it. One time I sent her downstairs with a bloody nose. I got the nickname Slugger. It was a pretty drug-crazed time in my life. Thank God I had my nephew Butch living with me. He stopped people from fucking my house up. I would go over to Harlow's, get wasted on Scotch, and when the club closed, I'd invite everybody back to my place. It's amazing nothing got smashed or stolen. I was enjoying this cocaine thing that I had discovered and not making great decisions about who I was partying with.

By the time we start the *Time's Makin' Changes* tour, I'm on coke like Jeff and Frank, and I'm thinking this is going to be great: I'm going on the road, we're going to snort a bunch of cocaine, play shows, fuck chicks. But Frank chose that time to quit. One day at our hotel, he called me and said, "Come over to my room." I go into his room, and there was this fucking big white boulder in his toilet.

I said, "What's that?"

He said, "That's my coke."

I'm like, "Why the fuck did you do that? You could have given it to me!"

Now it's just me and Jeff getting fucked up. Frank and Troy are sober, and there's a division between us. For the first time, Frank and I couldn't communicate. I think he was really disgusted because he had looked at me as the guy who kept it all together. Frank and Troy had had enough and didn't want to be there. Me, I really didn't want to accept that it was the end. I wanted to party through it, hoping we'd come out somewhere on the other side.

I'd already had a cocaine overdose. As soon as I bought the J Street house my mom started coming over, and I would torment her because I'd be fucked up. I'd come home from Harlow's, and she'd see me get sick. One time, I was home on a break from the tour. I'd snorted a bunch of blow and then went out to dinner with Dan McClendon. Obviously, I didn't eat. I just drank a lot of wine and ended up getting really ill. Dan took me home, and I couldn't quit throwing up. I started freaking out, thinking I was dying. My mom was staying that night, and I really felt bad because it scared her.

I called my friend's husband, a tattoo artist who was clean and sober, a good guy, and said, "Hey man, I think I overdid it. I think I'm ODing on blow and booze." He came over. My mom was trying to get me to go to the hospital, and I said, "No, I'll be all right," while my friend was trying to get me to check into a twenty-eight-day program.

He was saying, "Brian, you gotta go get some treatment, you're out of control."

I said, "I can't, man, I gotta go back on tour tomorrow. When I get back I promise I'll check into rehab." Of course, I never did. But that was the most fucked up I've ever been in my life. It was a depressing time.

TESLA DIED ONE NIGHT IN RENO. Towards the end of the tour, one of Jeff's ponies had died and when he heard about it, he had an emotional meltdown. Jeff is a real emotional guy, period. He likes animals better than humans. If he sees a homeless guy, he gets upset. He doesn't like to see the bad things that happen in the world. He wanted to go home, but our tour manager said, "Don't go home. We'll put you in a room for two days, don't talk to anybody, and you'll be able to finish the last three shows." He went home anyway, and I don't know if he did a ton of drugs, but when he came back for the show in Reno he was irrational, totally out of his mind. He was doing blow; I was doing blow. The drum tech was carving out lines for me and Jeff on CD cases between songs. I don't think he lost his voice from doing drugs, I think he lost his voice from crying about the horse. When he gets that way, he's hard to deal with.

After three songs, he went to sing and nothing came out. We just stopped playing. Jeff tried to tell the crowd that he's sorry he can't sing. He's crying. The crowd is booing and throwing shit at the stage. Jeff then collapses, and our wardrobe person has to carry him back to the dressing room. Troy's looking at me and saying, "Go up to the mic and say something!"

And I'm like, "I ain't saying shit. Fuck it, this thing's done!" We just straggled off the stage into the dressing room.

Even though I was fucked up, I felt I was doing my job, but now Jeff couldn't sing. This had been a long time coming, and I wasn't going to go out front and try and smooth things out with the audience. Jeff is having a breakdown and saying, "The band has ruined my life, I don't want to do it anymore, I quit." Frank and Troy said fuck it, they were tired of all the shit.

I said, "Guys, what are we doing? We're each making a hundred and fifty grand a year, let's not be stupid." They all yelled at me, so I said OK, fine, fuck it!

We headed back home, and I called up for another eight ball. Frank got back into the Peruvian marching powder as well. We didn't hear from Jeff at all. We didn't get the "I'm sorry" rap that we got before every time he threatened to quit. So after about five days, Frank and I started to get really pissed off and realized, *Fuck it, I guess we're really going to break up.* We called our lawyer, Peter Paterno, and said, "Dissolve Tesla, we're disbanding!" We didn't even call Troy, and he is resentful about that. He probably thinks he could have changed our minds.

Paterno called Jeff and said, "The band has broken up, you don't have a band anymore."

Then Jeff called me up crying and said, "Hey man, what's goin' on?"

And I said, "It's time to call it quits, it's not fun anymore." There was nothing he could do or say that could change things.

At that point Peter and Cliff also had had enough of our antics throughout the years. If Tesla were the biggest band on the planet, making millions of dollars, I think they would have flown out and gotten us together in a room, because it would be in their best interest. But because we had slipped down the ladder, I don't think it was worth the aggravation, and I can't really blame them, because it wasn't easy for those guys. They took a lot of abuse from us. After I dissolved the band, Cliff called me up, and I basically said, "Jeff's all fucked up. No one's getting along. It's not fun anymore. We're done!"

THE BAND BROKE UP IN 1995. Drugs and alcohol had a lot to do with it. I think one of the big reasons we were getting fucked up is because all of a sudden we felt no one wanted to listen to our music anymore, and that was painful. We thought it would last forever, but when grunge arrived, radio didn't want us anymore, and promoters didn't want to put us into ten-thousand-seat venues. We were selling out our gigs, but they were focusing on this new movement, and Tesla got put to the back of everyone's list. We weren't a priority for anybody. That's when the band got deeper and deeper into drugs. No one told us that this thing would decline, that music is cyclical. Cliff had a casual attitude about it. He was like, "Things have changed. It's over for you, just accept it."

I was like, "What? What do you mean it's over? Two years ago I was playing to twelve thousand people, what happened?"

Within a week of splitting up, Frank and I started what is now Soulmotor. We got Darin Wood in on vocals and started writing songs. For me it was a natural way to go. I had been in a band since I was eighteen; now I was thirty-two, and it's all I knew how to do: start a band, get a record contract, and pick up where we left off. But I was soon to realize that it wasn't that easy. Frank, Darin, and I did some demos, sent them out, and people weren't too keen on it. The songs were quite dark, and that kind of turned Frank off and he split.

Even though Frank quit, I spoke to him quite often. Out of the entire band, Frank and I are the closest. We spent the most time together in Tesla. We shared rooms, had sex with girls together;

we are like brothers no matter what happens with our work and careers. Frank really taught me how to play and is the yardstick I measure myself against. Frank was amazing when he was fifteen. I saw it then and knew I wanted to be in a band with him. After he left Soulmotor, Frank started Moon Dog Mane, Jeff and Tommy started Bar 7, and Troy started a roofing company.

I lost touch with Jeff for a couple of years. I was pissed off and hurt that Tesla had broken up, and I blamed Jeff for it. I would leave messages with his wife, but I never heard back. Coincidentally, when he got divorced, we hooked back up and started hanging out, shooting pool and stuff. He was in a lot better shape than at the end of Tesla. It was good to see him looking healthier. Maybe getting the divorce was not a coincidence.

The Soulmotor saga was like paying back taxes. Unlike Tesla, the first track we released didn't go through the roof. I was starting from a lower place than I had been before. The tour bus was replaced with a van pulling a trailer. We were playing to ten people some nights. Even though I had a new band, I really missed Tesla—going on tour, recording, and the adulation. Now that I was on my own, I was driven to get Soulmotor to be a band like that. I had to manage the situation.

All this responsibility was now on my shoulders. My anxiety was really getting on top of me. I had unrealistic expectations. I was financing it myself, and of course there was no Tesla touring money coming in, and royalties were slim, so it was really just money going out. I did everything I could to keep expenses down. I was driving the van. I was the manager and the booking agent, as well as bandleader and songwriter. Now I had this big house and a mortgage that went with it. While I was doing these little club tours in 1999, I went to a doctor because I was having trouble hearing. It was just a lot of wax buildup in my ear canals, but he also said my thyroid was swollen.

When I got home I went to see my doctor, Scott Staab. He ordered an ultrasound, and there were two nodules on my thyroid, which wasn't a good thing. The first thing you think of is cancer, right? Well, after some more tests and ultrasounds every month, the nodules just disappeared. That was good, but the tests also showed that my thyroid function was not normal. This was another symptom of the autoimmune disease. It wasn't a critical thing at that point, but of course the specialists wanted to put me on meds because that's the way the medical industry works. But Doctor Scott wasn't a typical MD and suggested we stop the meds and just keep monitoring the situation, so I've held off doing that all these years since.

About four months later my autoimmune system went haywire again, and I had a massive bout of colitis. The pain was almost unbearable, and I was shitting blood. Doctor Scott sent me to a gastroenterologist who gave me a colonoscopy. It was a bad case of colitis, and he put me on a course of Asacol, which helped, but the colitis would recur when the stress reached a trigger point, which at that time in my life there were a lot of. Fortunately, during all this I had health insurance as part of the Tesla partnership, and I still do, though the rates have gone up quite a bit.

The record company I eventually signed Soulmotor to in 1998, Sanctuary Records, wanted to put a "Featuring Brian Wheat of Tesla" sticker on the album, and I wouldn't let them do that. I wouldn't let them put Soulmotor records next to Tesla records in the stores. For me it was important that this was something new I was doing. I wanted to find a whole new fan base. I cut off all my hair when Tesla broke up. I really tried to shed my ties. Looking back, I don't think that was a good idea. The Tesla connection would have been good for Soulmotor and me personally. Instead of making it an extension, I tried to erase it. Tesla is a big part of who I am, though I wouldn't admit it.

I did feel more liberated with Soulmotor. Now I had a band where I had a lot more to say, and I didn't have to go to a committee of people. I was writing a lot more songs than I did with Tesla. It was liberating, but it wasn't paying the bills! The money I'd saved with Tesla I was using to fund Soulmotor. During this time I was kind of running a party house on J Street. Basically I had an underground tunnel running from Harlow's to my house. When Tesla broke up, there was a lot of cocaine consumed at my house, lots of Ecstasy, and lots of marijuana. The Lost Weekend lasted about a year and a half.

The sound of Soulmotor when Frank was in it is not the sound of the band now. Frank wasn't playing like he was in Tesla; we were kind of grungy, tuning down. We did some cool songs. There were two songs that wound up being on Soulmotor's first album that Darin and Frank and I did together, "Good Day to Die" and "Kali." Those were cool. Frank said it was too depressing for him. Darin had some pretty dark lyrics about coffins, worms, and dying. He was involved in those "zombie marches"; it's just where he came from. He is an artist, a good artist, and does all the Soulmotor artwork. The thing with Darin is we are buddies, and we work well together. Ever since we started in 1995, when we get together on a writing session, we'd finish that day with a song. We jibe. I let him do his thing, he lets me do my thing, and it works together. With Frank, I think he probably wanted to do his own thing, not be attached to me again. Soon after Frank left Soulmotor, he formed Moon Dog Mane.

I knew this amazing guitar player named Tommy McClendon who Frank and I grew up idolizing. He was Dan McClendon's brother and played in a Stockton band called Thunderwing. Tommy joined, and I think the first song we wrote together was "Guardian Angel" and a song called "Touch of Strange." We were like, "Wow, this is really cool," and that became the band, with Darren Minter on drums. That's the band that got the record contract. We had to get rid of Darren because he got too fucked up at a couple of showcases and blew one of them. Me coming out of Tesla, I had no tolerance whatsoever. It was like, that's it, you're gone. Then we got Mike Vanderhule on drums.

On the first Soulmotor release in 1999 we played a lot of dates. When time came to record the second album, *Revolution Wheel*, I called Troy to come up and play because Mike Vanderhule was getting on everyone's nerves. He's a nice guy, and I recommended him to Y&T when they were looking for another drummer, but he just didn't connect personality-wise with all of us. I'm hard on drummers anyway, so that had to end.

Troy came up for three weeks. We spent the first two weeks rehearsing and laid down his tracks the third week. This was in my house, with the drums in an upstairs parlor, and the control room next to it in a bedroom. I recorded everything in the house and mixed it in LA with this guy I met through Troy, Roger Summers. He had slipped me his reel at one of my house parties, and it was real contemporary stuff, exactly what was going on at rock radio at the time.

Tommy McClendon lost interest after the second record. One of the songs we wrote and demoed before he left was called "Down in Mexico." After *Revolution Wheel*, I thought that was it for Soulmotor. It was over six years before we made the album *Wrong Place at the Right Time*. I sent the demo to this guy, Blake, at WJJO in Madison, Wisconsin. They were big supporters of Soulmotor and had given "Guardian Angel" quite a bit of airplay. He loved it, so I called up Darin and said, "How would you like to make another Soulmotor album?" My friend, guitarist Mike Mathis, came up to Sacramento and brought his drummer with him, Dave Watts.

I had finally built my studio out in back of the house in a separate building. We recorded *Wrong Place at the Right Time* there with Terry Thomas mixing. We put the album out, and it didn't do that well. We did a proper radio campaign, and it just cost me a lot of money, paying independent radio promoters and so forth.

On the next Soulmotor album, *Box of Shadows*, which as of this writing is almost set to go, I want to go out and do a tour. On the album, I'm playing guitar to get the structure I want, then I have Dave Rude lay down some proper shit. It's good stuff, and I think it has an audience. I want to do a mixture of larger support gigs and smaller headline shows.

As I said, I was always against using the Tesla brand to support my individual projects, like "featuring Brian Wheat from Tesla." But at this point it's a useful thing to do, to bring in a younger audience, but still reference it to this other body of work. Darin has a following from his movies, so there's that group of fans as well. We won't be doing "Signs" though!

Soulmotor is a real band, not a project. It's like Steely Dan. It's a writing partnership. We've gone through several guitar players and several drummers, but Darin and I, since 1995, have stayed the same. If we were to go out on tour, we'd get a couple of hired guns and be in charge of the whole product. Dave Rude plays amazing on this new record. I plan on going out on tour with Dave, Darin, and Derek Diesen on drums, who was in this band I managed and produced called Built by Stereo. He's a great drummer. He's actually one of my favorite drummers, which isn't easy to be.

Like I said, I'm hard on drummers. I'm very particular. I think drummers tend to overplay and complicate things too much. Derek is really good in the sense that I'll write a drum part when Darin and I are writing songs, and then he adapts it. We just go into the control room, and I put up a drum loop and play my guitar or a bass, or a synth, or piano, and Darin sings the melody. That's how the songs start. I do write a lot of drum parts, and Derek's fine with it, and he plays them way better than what I write. He's the perfect drummer for me when I want to do something. He understands what I want and knows enough to improve things, not, "Let me change this," or "I would do it this way." I can't play the drums, or I would do them myself; that's really the point of it, for me. I can't play guitar like Dave Rude or Frank Hannon, or I'd do it myself, so on this album I took the approach of, "I'll play the scratch guitar, and they can play what I play."

Physically I was in good shape thanks to my wife, Monique. The night I met her, I had gone to Harlow's to look for some dope. I saw her across the room, and she came over. She had these tight white pants and an incredible ass. She said hello in this sexy Southern drawl. I asked her where she was from, and she said France. I said, "Really, what are you doing here?" She said she was a foreign exchange student, which was all bullshit; she was drunk. Anyway, she ended up being my buddy. She used to come around to my parties where thirty, forty people would be at the house. I think she just enjoyed watching the freak show.

I wanted to go out with her, but her roommate wanted to go out with me. Her name was Annie Rodman; she had been to married to Dennis Rodman, the basketball player. I didn't like Annie in that way; she just wasn't my type. I don't like blondes. She was buffed out, had short blond hair, and looked like Susan Powter. I had my sights set on Monique. But she said if I wanted to go out with her, I would have to quit being a dope fiend. I never did it around her, but she saw the aftereffects. So I said OK and I quit. We started hanging out, and then Annie found out. Monique called me up crying, saying that she couldn't see me anymore. I said, "Why?"

She said, "Annie says if I keep seeing you I gotta move out."

So I said, "Fuck it! Move into my pad," thinking that she'd move in for a couple of months, and it would be done, over. But it didn't work out that way. She moved in and hasn't left yet.

She's the one who straightened me out. After she moved in, all of my drug buddies would still want to come over and party, and she ran them all off. They'd come over at three in the morning with drugs and alcohol, and she'd say, "I'm asleep, you gotta go, you can't come in," right in their faces. Everyone was, "Hey dude, what's up with Mary Poppins, man?" All the guys who I was running with at that time quit coming around. Butch was still living there too. Monique loved Butch. Butch looked after her. He was downstairs, we were upstairs.

I was lucky to have Monique around to keep me grounded, because I can imagine it could have gotten worse. I could have gotten more and more into drugs. She just said, "Look dude, if I'm going to date you, you can't do drugs." She just wasn't into it. I was smitten by her. She never had done any drugs, still hasn't. Never smoked pot, never took a pill, and she just wasn't into it. She's got brothers, and I'm sure her brothers have done cocaine. Her one brother was a fuckup, and he got his life together, and he was in rehab. I didn't know that at the time. Maybe that's why Monique was so strict about the drugs. So, I thought, *OK, I'd like to date you. You're cute, you're nice. I don't have to do cocaine, I can stop*, and I stopped like that. She didn't care about the drinking; we'd both get fucked up. Wednesday, Thursday, Friday, Saturday, we were at Harlow's getting hammered upstairs, me and her. The first two or three years we were together, just getting fuckin' drunker than shit. That was OK, but no drugs.

For comparison purposes, I got to know Monique much better before commitment than I did Sandi. I lived with Monique for four years. I realized I needed to do that if I was going to make a commitment. I didn't want dogs in that house, and she's like, "I want a Jack Russell terrier."

I said, "No, no, no." Then she starts buying dog beds and dog dishes and shit, and I'm like, "What are you doing? I told you no." Next thing I know, we had Bonnie and Clyde.

She said, "Well I've got this dog on reserve, this little Jack Russell." Then we went to get Bonnie, and she came out and had a hernia, and I didn't like her. Bonnie wasn't very friendly.

Then they said, "Well, we've got one left, her brother Clyde," and he came running out and jumped on me.

He was licking my face, and I said, "Ah, this is the one we gotta get."

Monique said, "No, I want the female."

I said, "I want the male. I'll tell you what, you can have the female, but that male's my dog. If you ever leave, you're not taking my dog," because Sandi and I fought in court over our German shepherd for hours. That was the biggest battle in the whole divorce. My lawyer said, "Give her the fuckin' dog." Those were exactly her words, "Give her the fuckin' dog."

So Monique was living there; she kind of turned my house around. We shared the same bed, she was my girlfriend, lover, my better half. She started growing plants all over the place, inside, outside. All that greenery made the place feel alive and inviting. She straightened out the kitchen in a major way. We could actually find stuff when she got done.

I dated her for four years, and finally she kept saying, "We should get married."

I said, "Well, you know, I don't have a record contract. Wait till Soulmotor gets a record deal; I don't have an income." Mr. Practical.

Then Soulmotor got a deal, and she's like, "OK, marry me." I kept putting it off. I didn't want to get married, because I'd just gone through that divorce. We didn't talk about having kids; we never really thought about it. Monique took birth control, and she didn't want kids.

But I did say, "Well, if I'm going to marry you, you're going to have to sign a pre-nup."

She said, "No problem, I don't want your money." I didn't really have a bunch of money, but I had assets. You never know what the future is going to hold. So she didn't bat an eye, she signed it, and we amended it later. She never gave a fuck about the money; that always holds big cards for me. Bottom line is, "If I die, you get it all. If you leave for some fuckin' young dude with a big dick, you ain't getting shit, fuck off."

The Return of Tesla—
Why the Fuck Not?

In 1998, three years after Tesla split up, I had a New Year's Eve party and Jeff turned up. He'd cut all his hair off and looked really good. What I didn't realize was that he'd been in jail after being busted with crank. He got thirty days in the hole. Part of his sentence was that he had to do twelve-step meetings, stay clean and sober, and get piss tests. We were both sober for the first time in many years.

You could see he was lonely. I felt really bad for the guy. You could see that he had to deal with a lot of shit that he'd never dealt with before. It was like old times. If there were any weird vibes, it was over that night. We started hanging out together. I was keen to rekindle our friendship.

There's a radio disc jockey in Sacramento by the name of Pat Martin. He used to come around my house a lot and was really supportive of Soulmotor. He was always asking if I ever thought of getting Tesla back together, and at the beginning I would say, "Absolutely no fucking way!" Jeff was out with his band Bar 7 with

Skeoch, and Frank had his own band. We weren't mad at each other anymore. Eventually I was like, "Well, you never know, it could happen. If everyone was in agreement, I would do it."

One night Pat came over and said, "What would you say to Tesla playing at our big yearly radio festival?"

I said, "I'll tell you what. If they all say yeah, I'll do it. But it's got to be the original band, it's got to have Tommy Skeoch in it as well."

The thing is that Jeff was having the same problems with Tommy in Bar 7 that we had with him in Tesla. One day I get a call from Jeff about seven in the morning. I'm like "What the hell? Hey Jeff, what's up?" He's live on this radio station on the East Coast, which is three hours ahead.

He said, "Hey Brian, I need Frank's number!"

I said, "Get me off the radio and I'll talk to you." Tommy was all fucked up again, and Frank ended up playing on the last three weeks of a Bar 7 tour. When he got back, Frank told me that Jeff was still in good shape. So after hearing that, when Pat came around and asked about a reunion, I was much more open to doing it. He said that he wanted the band to do it at Arco Arena in Sacramento. I said, "Dude, that's like eighteen thousand people. I don't know if we can do four thousand people." We'd been away for almost five years.

He said, "Trust me, if you get back together, you will be able to sell out the arena."

All I could say was, "You're fucking nuts!"

In the meantime, Jeff was getting married again. He asked me if I knew who did this song called "I Love You," and he sang a bit over the phone. There might be two dozen songs with that title, but I thought it could be one by the Climax Blues Band. Jeff said, "Yeah, that's the one. I want to play that at my wedding."

I said, "Tell you what, I've got a proper studio now. I'll get Frank and Troy, and you can sing it; your wife will love it!" So that's what we did for our first get-together, and we wound up putting it on the *Twisted Wires* album.

Everyone agreed to do the show, and after a few phone calls we scheduled a rehearsal. We did the first two days without Jeff, as he was in England doing press interviews for Bar 7. The first two nights were just the four of us. The first song we played was "EZ Come EZ Go." After the last note faded out, we were jumping up and down, high fiving each other. It sounded like we'd never stopped playing. When Jeff got back, we rehearsed for a couple of weeks. We did an in-store appearance, and two thousand people showed up. All the local news stations were running stories about Tesla getting back together for one night, and sure enough, we came close to selling out the arena.

It was a pretty highly charged night. It was heavy seeing all these people come out who weren't there in '95 when grunge happened, and there was this love and support for Tesla. It was really emotional for me; I started crying before the first song. They were running this film going through the history of the band. We were in the back, and you could hear the whole arena rumbling, and it was like, "Oh my god!" None of us had felt that since we broke up. We did the show, which was good, and then we went back to my house and had a party. Tom Zutaut turned up; there were a lot of good vibes in the room.

While we were rehearsing, Jeff came over to me and said, "Maybe we should do some shows. Let's go out for two or three weeks. We could all use some money." I was cool with that. I was getting ready to make the second Soulmotor album at the time, so I was up for it. We agreed to do a three-week tour. We put the tickets on sale and quickly sold out every show. After that we thought, *Fuck it! Let's be a band again. Why not?*

It was that simple. All it took was doing a show, and someone extending an olive branch. We weren't pissed off with each other anymore, and everyone was up for it. You would hope that everyone was over the silly bullshit that broke the band up in the first place, the drugs and acting stupid. Some of us had spent and lost their money. To have that taken away was a very humbling experience. You realized that you weren't the shit. You were just in a band, and you were lucky to have a career that lasted that long and still have a fan base that would support you. Unfortunately, later in the story it becomes apparent that one of us never got it.

I called Cliff Burnstein and said, "Hey, Tesla is back together, are you interested?"

He said, "No, I'm not into nostalgia."

I said, "OK."

Then I asked Mensch if he was interested, and he said, "If you write great songs I might be."

I was like, "Didn't we write great songs before?"

He said, "You gotta write great songs now." Thompson and Barbiero said the same thing. I thought when we put the band together that we'd go back to Bearsville, like the first record, and the whole team would be ready to go. I quickly learned that they weren't ready to go because they didn't give a shit.

We tried a few managers, but no one could manage the band the way I wanted it to be done. The problem was that I had learned too much through the years and was having to tell managers what to do. If I had to tell them what to do, why should I be paying them? Any new manager who came in on the backs of Peter and Cliff was making money on something that was established fifteen years before. They're not looking at what the band needs to do now that's new, or creative ways to repackage us. None of them thought like that.

When we were on tour, the famed record executive John Kalodner turned up one night and asked us to sign with him and Sony Records. I'm like, "Why should we sign with you when we can do it ourselves and make six dollars a record versus your two dollars?"

He went, "You know you're right, you could do that, but you wouldn't have the machine of Sony Records behind you."

I'm like, "What's the machine going to do for us?" These guys wanted to put us out with the old bands, and Tesla wanted to be associated with groups like the Black Crowes.

There had been a formal dissolution of our relationship with Q Prime some years prior. Tesla, the partnership, always owned our logo, the brand, the symbols, the icons, the unique spelling of the word Tesla, all that stuff; we still do. I guess that's something that doesn't necessarily always happen, so, to Peter and Cliff's credit, they made sure that we owned that stuff going forward, even when they weren't going to be involved. It wasn't like we had to re-invent our brand.

They had a long sunset clause in the contract, a slow fade-out of their commission. We paid them, and I don't begrudge paying them; they earned every dime they ever got from us. I was a little disappointed that they didn't want to work with us again, but that was just natural because I thought they were the best, and I still think they're the best, but I'm over it. I wouldn't want to work with them today.

We needed to hire another lawyer, and we went back to Peter Paterno. We went back to his office, but we didn't have him, we had his underlings, and they put us all back together like Humpty Dumpty. We're back up in it now, and the machine's been running for seventeen years. Longer than the first time around—almost twice as long. It happened so quick, the first time around. That's what the machine can do when it chooses.

It's become a career now; it wasn't a career back then. It's funny, every night on stage Jeff says we've been together thirty years, thirty-one years, minus those four bad years that we were apart. We've learned now how to cohabitate, and if we get on each other's nerves, we don't want to break up; it's like, "Look, we're going to do this 'til we fuckin' die."

I was talking to Tom Lipsky, who had signed Soulmotor to Sanctuary Records, and I said, "Tesla is back, would you be interested in doing a record? I want a fifty-fifty deal on the royalties."

He said, "Yeah, I'll do that." He came out to see us, and we ended up doing a two-record deal. One was a double album called *RePlugged Live,* which started out as a live album, but everyone kept going into the studio and fixing and re-recording things. It came out on September 11, 2001. What a day to release a record, right?

The rationale behind *RePlugged* was to celebrate getting back together and to make up for the fact that we had never done a proper live album. It was a great idea. We should have thought, "We're back together, it would be cool to put out an album of the live reunion, not a quick product that we rush out." But we didn't think like that. I think like that, but as a group, we don't. *The Five Man Acoustical Jam* was so raw, and so attractive because of that, but *RePlugged* couldn't stay that way. I think it was because some of the guitars started to sound out of tune, and then Roger Summers was there, and he didn't come from the Tesla school, so he had kind of planted in our brain that we needed to make this sound amazing. We should have stuck to our guns. Look what happened with *Five Man Acoustical Jam.*

Troy was like that too. Troy's never liked a record we made until ten years later. It's like, "That record didn't sound good," then ten years later he'll tell me how amazing it is. That's just Troy's character; he was on the negative thing. Jeff didn't want to re-sing anything, and they kind of made him re-cut some vocals. We recorded a bunch of different shows, and then Troy got involved because he was worried about his drum tracks, picking songs because it was a good drum performance instead of a good band performance. He was too focused on what he was doing. We were letting Troy take the reins, and that was a bad move.

We should have just picked the best performances, which is what we did on *Mechanical Resonance Live*. Frank and I picked the performances, and I mixed them. We just told Troy, "Here it is." We didn't care if the drums were great, as long as the performance on the whole was good. All Troy cared about was the drums. He said, "The drums were great. You guys can overdub." That's where that whole overdub train of thought came from on *RePlugged Live*. We should have just found the tape that was, on the whole, good, even if the drums weren't perfect. It was all based around Troy's drums. Sometimes he gets into these things, and we allowed him to get into it. It's as much our fault for allowing it as it is his for suggesting it. We could have said no, but we were trying to be all peace and love, "Hey, we're all back together, let's respect and love one another," all that happy horseshit, instead of doing what was right. I'm always preaching, "Let's do the right thing no matter what." If there's three out of five in favor of it, that's what we need to do. Not this unanimous decision, 'cause it wasn't unanimous. I can't listen to *RePlugged*; it's terrible sounding, it's all high end, it's not live, that wasn't the real performance. There was other stuff that we recorded that was better.

After the album was finally put together, we just kept touring to support it. Next we started working on our comeback album, *Into the Now*.

Now I had added all this Tesla responsibility and stress to go along with the Soulmotor load. I had occasional bouts of colitis, some worse than others. When a particularly bad episode flared up, the gastroenterologist put me on prednisone, which is a synthetic steroid. I was on that for three months, and in that time, I gained about fifty pounds. I didn't really think about the weight gain or connect it with the prednisone, it just seemed to be there one day.

Although Tesla was back together, it didn't mean the situation was stable. It was quite the opposite, actually. We still had our big egos and demons, and I always felt like the rug could be pulled out from under me at any time. One big argument had done it in the past, and that could be all it would take now.

So I'm doing this balancing act between having colitis attacks or being on the miracle weight-gain drug prednisone. Both sides sucked. On top of that I was still drinking heavily, partly as an escape, partly because I'd quit doing drugs, and a young man just has to have a go-to vice. Mine was Scotch.

DURING THIS TIME STEVE CLAUSMAN was married to a woman named Rosie. His health was in decline, and he had a couple of bad incidents, a couple of open-heart surgeries. He was laid up in his living room for a long time, hooked up to tubes that were pumping juice through him and electrodes exercising his muscles. Steve's kind of a tough guy to live with, and when he got back on his feet, Rosie couldn't take it anymore. In 2002 Steve called me and said, "Rosie threw me out, and I'm sleepin' on this guy's couch." Monique and I used to hang with Steve and Rosie all the time; they'd come by when they were in Sacramento.

I said, "We can't have him sleeping on that couch. If it wasn't for him, we wouldn't be in this house with all this shit." So I told him he could come move in with me and Monique, and he stayed about a year and a half.

Steve always had a tendency to rule over whatever situation he was in. He cut down some of Monique's camellias, and it was game on. You don't mess with Monique's garden. He went out there one day and decided they needed trimming. It pissed her off, but she loved him and he loved her.

"You know," his son Brian had told me, "Hide your Home Depot card if Pops moves in with you. He'll piss you off sooner or later." It was no big deal to me, but it was a big deal to her.

Then he started rearranging the kitchen. That was Monique's territory as well, and I told Steve, "Hey bro. You gotta go live in Southern California, down to Brian's place in Newport Beach."

We loved him like a dad. His diabetes got bad. There were a couple of times when he lived with us and he had attacks; he was starting to lose toes. They were cutting this toe off and that toe off. His health was deteriorating, he got tired, and I think he threw in the towel. To be honest, I think he just said fuck it, went in hospice, and said, "I'm not taking any more medication." He literally got tired of being sick all the time and on medication. I think everybody's got a certain point they set in their head and say, "If it gets to this, that's it." It was weird because that whole last week, when he was doing so bad, he wouldn't talk to me; I couldn't get him on the phone. We were going to go down and see him. I don't think Steve could do it. It was too much for him. He died on his son Brian's birthday.

I'd speak to Brian every day, "What's going on with your dad," this, that, and the other. The old man was the closest thing I had to a dad, outside of my godfather when I was a kid. I wanted to please him, and I was happy when he was proud of something I'd done. It's that kind of thing. I could tell that he was proud of me and what I did. He and I had a pretty interesting relationship. One time he pissed me off and I said, "You ever wonder why you've been married five times? Did you ever think maybe it was you?" I could get in his ass, and he would listen, but that took years and years and years. But we loved him, especially Frank and I, till the day he died, the old dude. He'd come and see us play in LA.

We cried when he left. When he was here, he just hung out. He was past that stage of going out to look at bands; he would play me stuff in his room and say, "Hey, come listen to this." He didn't go out. When he came to live with us, it was the last part of his life. The dogs, Bonnie and Clyde, loved him. Clyde always used to piss on his bedroom door because Steve wouldn't let Clyde into his room. Steve was kind of finicky about how he had his room and stuff. So Bonnie and Clyde had a little bed in the kitchen, and his bedroom was right next to the kitchen, and he would shut the door, and Clyde would piss on it.

I remember one time I was in Italy and I called him. He's like, "That fuckin' Clyde."

I'm like, "What happened?"

He goes, "That fucker pissed in front of my door. I went out to get a drink of water, and I slipped and fell on my fuckin' ass right in the middle of the fuckin' kitchen."

I said, "Clyde was saying, 'Fuck you, you're not going to let me in the fuckin' bedroom, I'll piss on your door.'" Clyde pissed on a lot of stuff. He was my boy.

Steve taught me, Frank, and Jeff how to work. When we were under him, man, we were rehearsing eight hours a day, five days a week, cutting his fuckin' grass, raking his leaves. You'd go up there and live with him, and he'd feed you, and he taught you, "Nothing's free in life." He was into mentoring people. I think he was a good mentor. I never really talked to him about business. When I first met him, we all thought he was rich, and the next thing you know he's fuckin' broke and living up in Foresthill. So I don't really think he was a businessman. He said, "I've been rich and poor three times in my life." Well, that's not good business. What did he see in City Kidd that was special? He saw Jeff Keith; he knew Jeff Keith was a star. He knew Frank was a star, and he was absolutely right about it. He could see talent. He couldn't really put his finger on how to describe it or whatever, but anyone he ever worked with, I understood why he worked with them. He saw something in them. He could have been a great talent scout because he could recognize raw talent, he just couldn't develop it. He would piss people off because he was so blunt and acted like he was a drill sergeant. When you're a young kid that doesn't go down too well, but you need that.

We didn't appreciate it at the time, but we do now, especially me and Frank; we dealt with him more than anyone. Jeff was there, but he didn't spend as much time with Steve as we did, and certainly didn't spend the time with Steve after we fired him like Frank and I did. We both say that a lot of who we are is because of Steve Clausman. In some sense, he's a little like a Brian Epstein. He saw things in us but didn't know quite how to relate to any of it. I think he had the heart of an entrepreneur; he wanted to be his own guy, his own boss, even if it cost him.

I think once he got a bunch of money, he got kind of wild. I remember when he had two Porsche 928s, he'd give you the keys and say go take a ride, bring it back tomorrow, crazy stuff. But you don't get that and then lose it by having good business sense. He was up and down a lot. But he was a generous motherfucker. He would take whole bands out to dinners and get you hookers. He was good hearted.

I knew a side of him from living with him when I was a kid, then a real vulnerable side of him when he lived with me the last part of his life. When City Kidd was working with him, we were his family. Jeff and I stayed up in Foresthill. We were up there doing household chores, and then going to Auburn, to our rehearsal place. That's how we worked our rent off. He taught us there's a price for everything, you have to work. We didn't mind. I remember being sick and having to go to the doctor. He was like, "Go to the doctor." I didn't pay for it, he did. I didn't have health insurance. He was good like that.

11

Into the Now

We started working on writing *Into the Now* in 2003. The difference between *Bust a Nut*, which was rooted in the classic Tesla sound, and *Into the Now* was huge. We realized that times had changed, so how were we gonna approach this? Stay loyal to the original Tesla sound and not gather any new audience, or do we try to be more contemporary and risk alienating our core following?

We said, "Look, it's 2003, we need to make a record that sounds like Tesla in 2003, not like Tesla in 1987 or even 1994. Let's experiment, listen to what's going on around us sonically— the arrangements." Everybody was thinking that way, nobody was saying nah, nah. We went into this warehouse where Frank had recorded some demos on his sixteen-track tape machine. Roger Summers, who had just finished mixing *Revolution Wheel*, wanted to work with us, and I thought he was quite good. He had also mixed *RePlugged Live*. The problems I had with that album were all about the recording, not the mixing. We started with him, but it didn't pan out. He didn't get the dynamic of Tesla and how it worked. We found out he was a bit of a high-strung guy, and we needed some-one mellow to counterbalance our hyperactiveness.

We called engineer/producer Michael Rosen. He was at Fantasy Studios producing Rancid while we were there working on *Bust a Nut*. The guys in Rancid raided our candy and snack stash one day when we weren't recording. We went over to their room the next day and screamed at Michael. That's how we met.

He came up to Sac with Pro Tools. We had never worked with Pro Tools. It had always been analog tape and we thought, *OK, this is going to be trippy*. We set up shop in Frank's warehouse in Pollock Pines, a little town up in the foothills east of Sacramento, and did the record on our own with Michael engineering it. We never brought in a producer. We had a blast. Michael had a great collection of microphones. At the same time, I was building my own recording studio, so when I wasn't working on tracks, I was home working on that. We recorded the album over the course of four months and then mixed it at my studio while the recording room was still being built.

We felt like we had something to prove, that we still had what it takes, that we were still viable. I think we always did better work when we felt that way. Even though we agreed we need to make a contemporary album, we didn't all agree on what "contemporary" should sound like. But we approached it with a spirit of compromise, and I think the end result reflects the best of what we were at that time.

Frank contributed the lion's share of musical ideas. He was really rolling, and we all saw it, so we just let him bring it. I was coming off five years of work with Soulmotor and was having a hard time redirecting myself into the Tesla song landscape. My ideas at the time were just too heavy, maybe too dark. I did bring "What a Shame" into the sessions, but other than that, I knew that Frank was nailing it, one foot in the classic Tesla sound and one foot in something contemporary, so it was all good. Jeff was really on his game with the lyrics as well.

Michael Rosen and I spent two weeks on the mixes, and no one liked them. Troy said, "You have to tune your room," because someone had told him that was what you did. Well, show up to the sessions and put your two cents in then. So Frank and Troy came down, and we re-mixed, and they were happy. I think *Into the Now* is one of our best. We were recharged, inspired, and happy to be in each other's company.

I have to mention here that we went to a psychiatrist before we recorded the album because we were having problems as a band. He was the psychiatrist I was seeing for my anxiety disorder. I went to the band and said, "Hey, Metallica is seeing a shrink, maybe we should, too, because we're having problems trying to get ready to do this album together. There are things we want to say to each other that we can't say. We don't know how to say them without pissing each other off, offending one another. We need a mediator."

There was an incident when we started writing songs for the album where Troy and I got into this huge fight. He said some really fucked up shit to me, and I didn't want to work with him anymore. He said I sucked as a bass player. I don't know why he said it. He'd done this to me before in the early days.

We went to the psychiatrist to smooth things out because I was like, "Fuck you, Troy." This wasn't the Troy that I made a record with in Soulmotor; that was a pleasurable experience. Now we're back in Tesla, and he's turning into this fucking dickhead and focusing it on me. I wasn't having any of it. I said to the band, "Are you OK getting some therapy so we don't end up breaking up again before we've even started?" We did that for about four months, and it got us focused.

The psychiatrist said, "Everything is going to be spinning round and round except your CD unless you get it together. You should not be taking alcohol or drugs if you want to get back together." Our basic rule was no hard drugs, no cocaine. If you want to smoke some weed or have a few drinks, go ahead.

We wrapped the album and went out to headline some shows. We were then set to go out with the Scorpions on tour. But at the end of those headline shows, Tommy had to go back into rehab. Frank, Jeff, and Troy came to me when we started the Scorpions tour in 2004 and said, "To help Tommy, we think we should all be sober."

I said, "I'm not doing it, I don't have a problem."

They said, "OK, if you don't want to, we understand."

I'm like, "I'm not fuckin' up. I'm not missing anything. I'm not missing gigs. I'm not playing bad. I have a couple of scotches a night. He's got the problem; why should I get sober for him?"

Then two days later I thought, "I'm the guy that's always preaching 'be a team,' 'one for all, all for one.'" That's when I stopped drinking, on that tour. We took all the alcohol off the rider, even the crew couldn't have any, because they rode on the bus with us. It was the best tour we ever had with Tommy.

We put out *Into the Now,* and the first single was a ballad, "Caught in a Dream." We sold forty-five thousand records in the first week and entered the charts at thirty-one. There was a lot of good buzz around the band. We went out and started touring these two- to three-thousand-seat halls. We were out there doing it again. The perception of us being a hair band from the '80s was gone. We were credible again.

We weren't financially better off, but we were making a lot more money from touring than we ever had. We got this guy, Steve Emler, who still works for us, in as a soundman/tour manager, and he brought to our attention how much money we were wasting on the road on our earlier tours where there were four buses, and everybody had a hotel room every day. Now we were doing it more compact, and we were keeping more money.

We started playing more shows, and Tommy Skeoch got up to his old tricks again. He started acting weird, doing things even he wouldn't normally do, like putting a dog collar on, getting on his hands and knees, and asking me to walk him around Manhattan on a leash, which I thought was hilarious. Troy didn't think it was funny, and neither did Jeff. But I was like, "Sure, I'll walk you around," because at this time Tommy and I were buddies again.

We were playing a show at Irving Plaza in New York, the same day he had me walk him with a leash, and we had all the Sanctuary Records people there. Tommy's not playing well, and Troy's going mental, saying, "Skeoch's on the pills!" while we're onstage.

I'm like, "No he's not, man, just be cool."

Troy replies, "Fuck you! He's on pills!" Then Tommy and Troy get into this big brawl backstage. Tommy said he wasn't high, Troy said he was, and no one really knew. The people from Sanctuary saw the fight, and that was the end of the support on that record.

We continued on the tour, and next thing we're in Reno. Now Tommy's really doing weird shit, wearing pink cowboy hats and drinking heavily. After the show we're on the bus, and he comes up to me and says, "Brian, I've been really bad." I asked him what he meant by "being bad." He said, "I've been taking pills, man."

I said, "Tommy, this is no good. You know you're not supposed to do that. Just go to bed, and we'll talk tomorrow." From that point on he kept taking pills and started to become as obnoxious as he had been when we got rid of him in 1995.

We played a big festival for this radio station in Chicago, and Tommy's just out of it; he can't play. So we finished the show, got him on the bus, and said, "Tommy, you're out of the band, and someone's going to replace you. You have one of two choices. You either go to rehab, sort yourself out, and come back, or we're going to look for somebody else." He chose rehab.

In the meantime, we got a friend of Frank's—Scott Johnson, a local Sacramento guy—to come in and play the remainder of the tour. He was a nice guy, but he wasn't *the* guy.

When the Scorpions tour finished, we decided to do an acoustic tour of the States, and Tommy starts fucking up again—taking pills. He consumed our manager's time, and instead of focusing on Tesla, our manager felt his job was to keep the five of us together and Tommy sober. So after that tour we started seeing a lot of Tom Zutaut, and he said we should go into the studio and record some acoustic songs. We were supposed to have a meeting with Tom in Chicago while we were touring with Def Leppard. We turned up at this restaurant, and Tommy is loaded on smack, nodding out. The guys are looking at me, Zutaut's looking at me, and I'm looking at Sterling, our manager, shaking my head and thinking, *This is enough!*

After a set one night, Tommy and I get into the dressing room, and I confront him about his using. He starts yelling at me. I picked him up and threw him into the lockers and yelled, "Motherfucker, I'll beat your ass!" I turned to the band and said, "I'll tell you what, I'll just split, and Tommy can stay in the band."

Tommy apologized and went back into rehab again. He joined us on the Canadian leg of the *Five Man Acoustic* tour in 2005. I think someone bought him a cake because he was supposed to be thirty days sober, but he was all fucked up. I just told him, "You might be bullshitting these guys, but you're not bullshitting me. You're finished!" Now I was super stressed with Tesla. I had this massive flare-up with my colitis and almost couldn't make the Canadian tour because I was in so much pain.

At that point Tom Zutaut was telling us we should start our own label. We went into the studio and started recording the material that was going to become *Real to Reel*. That's when Tommy started having problems again. At that point we decided we were going to take six months off, we're not going to do anything, and let Tommy get his shit together.

Sterling didn't do anything for us during those six months. There was nothing set up or anything, and everyone was pissed off. So Sterling got fired. He said, "You said you were taking six months off."

And I said, "We were taking six months off. We weren't expecting you to take six months off; we were expecting you to have gigs ready for us when we got back."

Out went Sterling Bacon. Because we were in with Tom Zutaut, who was kind of acting as our guru, producing these tracks that were going to end up being *Real to Reel* and helping to start our own record label, he said, "I can manage you. I know how to manage a band." OK. Sure. Why not! We didn't see a resume of his management background, but we trusted Tom. We'd known him our whole lives; we wouldn't be sitting here without him. Then it was Tom managing, and I was helping him, and I wasn't getting fuckin' paid.

After the tour we went into my studio to record some acoustic songs, and sure as hell Tommy is up to his old tricks. Once he started missing conference calls with management, we told Tommy we were going to piss test him, and he turned in a dirty test. He copped to it and said he had a vasectomy and got a bunch of pills for the pain. That was bullshit, and we'd had enough. I'd had a vasectomy, and I didn't take a bunch of pills, I just put a bag of frozen peas on my balls. So it was unanimously decided that he be asked to leave. Either that or the band was going break up again. The band couldn't tour because of Skeoch. People weren't going to have the ability to earn money to feed their families.

Predictably, the stress of Tommy leaving and the uncertain future that pointed the band towards triggered another onset of my colitis. As bad as the pain was, I was more affected by the prednisone, which kept packing on the pounds. I'd lose weight while the colitis was in charge and then put it on, and more, when I was on the drug. I've been losing and gaining the same forty pounds for years. On top of that, I developed a case of gout, which was like having arthritis in my joints. As some kind of coping mechanism, I began to eat more. My weight was now maxing around 250, and coupled with the gout, moving around onstage like I always had was all but impossible. No leaping off the drum riser anymore.

After Tommy exited, we started looking for a new guitarist. Frank saw this picture of Dave Rude on Myspace and thought he looked really cool with the scarves and crazy shit. That was just like it was with Tommy and Nasty Habits. "That guy looks cool," that's exactly what it was. Frank contacted Dave and asked him to come up from Oakland and have a jam, and then brought him out to my studio to record something. I stuck my head in the session and could tell he was really good. Frank took him out on a tour with the Frank Hannon Band, and he played a bunch of Tesla material there. We knew that this was the guy. He showed up for rehearsals and fit like a glove.

WE WENT OUT THAT SUMMER, played fairs, festivals, and got Dave into the groove of Tesla. We had started recording an acoustic album in the studio. Tom Zutaut had said, "Let's go record you acoustically in the studio because people really like that." It was all Tom's idea. Tom liked covers, and Tesla liked doing them. "Lil' Suzi" was a cover and so was "Signs." We would practice songs at sound check and play some in the show. Tom and I went to the South by Southwest music festival to sort out the best distribution deal for Tesla. We settled with Ryko, and they liked the covers album idea. For us it was about getting the band to do something positive and fun and also break in Dave Rude to see how he worked in the studio.

Pat Schneider, who helped build both my studios, knew about this place in West Texas. It was real old school, Neve desk, no automation, no Pro Tools. It was outside of El Paso, right on the Rio Grande river. In 2006 we went down there to this studio called Sonic Ranch for a month. We would pick a song, learn it, and record it. We had a blast. I think Tom's thinking was to recreate a time when we were a garage band starting out playing Def Leppard covers. The spin on it was that we only wanted to do older songs and do it on analog tape. We set some boundaries and said, "Let's pretend we're back in 1975 and only use the technology from that era." We mixed by hand. We really got inspired by that, and it's still a fun listen. We wound up doing two records, *Real to Reel Volume 1* was a regular release, and *Volume 2* initially was only given out as part of the ticket when you came to see us live.

The studio owner had a big pecan orchard that went right up to the river. The studio had big windows facing Mexico, and while we were laying down tracks we could look out and see Mexicans running through the orchard to get into the US and the immigration cops chasing 'em down. They were hiding behind trees; it was trippy. A lot different than Manhattan for sure.

I really loved how we went retro on those two albums, but it's not practical to make studio albums that way in this day and age. You have to compete in a world of modern technology, and all the advancements in the last forty years are there for a reason. It's like race cars. Richard Petty in a '75 Chevy couldn't compete in today's NASCAR, no matter how great he is.

We went on tour to support *Real to Reel,* and it was cool. We sold about eighty thousand copies of each album, which was on our own label. We got a lot of airplay on the lead track, which was Led Zeppelin's "Thank You." It was great, but also this is where we banged heads with Zutaut. Tom was very good at motivating the band. It was like the schoolmaster and his kids; the guy could have been a psychologist. It was also fun rekindling our relationship. He was the one who talked us into forming our own label and doing things on our own. Tom brought a lot of good things to the table. But managing Tesla is a hard job. There are four very strong personalities, and I probably know too much for my own good compared with the average musician. I know the mechanics of why everything happens. With Tom there's never been a problem from an A&R point of view, but when it got to managing the personalities and budgets, that wasn't his forte. His strength is finding a young, undeveloped band and turning them into Guns N' Roses, Tesla, or Mötley Crüe. Also he came from a school where David Geffen would give him a checkbook and say, "Spend what you need." With Tesla now operating as a cottage industry, there was no longer an unlimited checkbook. We had two different ways of thinking, and it didn't work out.

Once we got out on the road with him, we wound up going in debt for the first time touring. That had never happened before. I saw red. I was frustrated because he was putting a big workload on me, and I wasn't getting anything from it, not monetarily or anything, and I was running my immune system down. I said, "Wait a minute, you're the manager." Even Frank said Brian didn't do this with Peter and Cliff.

We were hemorrhaging money because he had no idea how to tour on a budget. Bad management, that's what it was. He wasn't a manager. Steve Emler always had good advice; he would say, "Look, you guys are losing money here," and I was seeing the weekly reports where we were spending all the money, and finally we just said enough is enough. So he got fired in Nashville. We're still great friends, still brothers. I talk to him all the time. He's going to move to Texas, hopefully here in Baird. I fired him, the band supported me in firing him, but we recovered from that because we're brothers. We love each other, the band still loves Tom, he's still part of our family.

Me at around seven years old.

My first bass and amp, at fourteen.

The man who got Tesla our record deal
and burned our serious work ethic into
us—Steve Clausman.

My godfather, Cecil Cayocca.

With my mom, Amelia, the night I got my first gold record

My best friend—my oldest brother, Buddy.

The Wheat family. In the back (L-R) are my brothers, David, Buddy, (me), and Mike. In the middle is my mother, Amelia, and my sister, Sheri. In front are my brother, Timmy, and my nephew, Butch.

With my first manager, Peter Mensch, a very important guy in my life.

My old pal, the late, great Steve Clark from Def Leppard.

With Ross Halfin at the Hammersmith Odeon, London, 1987.

My closest friend in any other band, Joe Elliott.

The time I met Paul McCartney, London, 1987.

My special home for thirty years on J Street, Sacramento.

Green Bay, Wisconsin, 1988, on the Hysteria Tour with Def Leppard.

Backstage at the Hammersmith Odeon, 1991. Photo by Ross Halfin.

With Dave Rude on the Styx/Tesla tour, 2018. Photo by Oliver Halfin.

With my traveling partner and partner-in-crime, Ross Halfin, Burma.

Above are Clyde and Bonnie, and below, Darla and Spanky.

Our newest set of Jack Russells: Louise, Alfalfa, and Thelma.

My brother from another mother, Brian Clausman

My "little brother" who taught me how to play bass. We started this journey together— Frank Hannon.

With Tesla drummer, Troy Lucketta.

With Dean "Jimmy Dean" Robson.

One of my art shows for the Wentworth Gallery.

Probably my most trusted helper; like a son to me, Brett "Lipps" Stetzel

Peter Torza, Monique, and me at Harlow's, 1995.

Such a pretty girl. My wife, Monique.

The two most beautiful women on the planet, Monique, and my former wife, Sandi.

SoulMotor, (L-R) Darin Wood, Tommy McClendon, and yours truly.

The one and only, Jeff. I love you to death, man.

Because we were friends it turned into this ugly blowout. I didn't talk to him for six months. There were some harsh words at the time. His daughter wrote all kinds of nasty shit about me on the internet, which was hurtful. The first thing I wanted to do was write back and say, "Fuck you, bitch!" but I never said anything. Tom didn't say anything, and out of respect for Tom I didn't say anything about what his daughter said. He should have, but I don't know if he ever did. She never apologized for it. I've forgiven her for it and have talked to her a couple of times. He was having me produce her, and she's talented, but too much drama. Tom and I never wrote anything bad about each other, we're fine. Maybe now he's learned how to manage somebody on a budget.

We were a week into the *Real to Reel* tour when Tom left, and everything was up in the air. We were supposed to go to England and play for the very first time in sixteen years, and nothing was sorted out. The band came to me and said, "Why don't you manage us, Brian? You've been doing it all these years. You were always the go-to guy with Peter and Cliff. You were the guy that networks with people." At that point we were picking up the pieces. We were in recovery mode, I just kept running the campaign. I have to say it was nice to get the 15 percent manager's fee, but I also know that I earned every fuckin' penny.

Even when Frank and I started City Kidd I was the contact guy. When Cliff and Peter were managers, they always dealt with me, and I always caught a lot of shit from the band for it. They said I was management's boy. But I was the guy they dealt with because they probably thought I was the most logical. I learned a ton of stuff from them as far as how to conduct oneself. Today, if I need managerial advice, I'll still call them.

We kind of got through all that, took a deep breath, and said, "Ok guys, it's time to make a new studio record." We'd done a record with Dave Rude and knew he could play. Dave's really easy to get on with. He doesn't have any baggage, no drug problems, no drama, no ego, no chip on his shoulder. He's just a pleasure to be around. Dave was a shot in the arm for the band. He was twenty-nine when he joined and lowered the average age of Tesla by about five years. He was a perfect fit for us. Everyone loves and respects the guy. He's a great guitar player. Every night he and Frank do this spontaneous jam, and you'd think they'd been playing together their whole careers.

Forever More or Less

By 2007 the industry had completely changed. The one thing I feel we never got a fair shot on with Sanctuary was being able to take a song and work it like a single should be worked—getting airplay on new outlets, creating innovative promotions, trying to broaden our audience, stuff like that. They were working Tesla based on the laurels, not our new music. Now, having our own label, we didn't have to ask anyone to do this. We could spend money where we wanted to on the tracks we wanted to and not have to get approval from some fuckin' record company.

When we were on tour in England in 2007, we reconnected with Terry Thomas. He came to a few gigs, and everybody was happy to see him. So I asked him if he would be up for doing another Tesla record, one where we wouldn't be all fucked up, out of our minds, and falling apart. He was up for it, so we started working on demos for *Forever More*. We were writing and recording at the same time, and it took five months to make. At this time Jeff was preoccupied with problems with his second wife and not contributing much to the writing process, but I don't think anybody was tripping on it. Terry co-wrote all the songs with us. At this point we didn't care where the songs came from as long as they were great.

Hindsight being twenty-twenty, the only problem from a financial point of view was that writing songs in the studio can be expensive. I love working from scratch, but it can be costly, and when you get into running your own label you've got to do things with a budget in mind. Today I'm very conscious about the money we're spending. We did spend some time writing and rehearsing before we went into the studio, but it was nothing like the old days when we had every note basically finalized. That's not to say that things wouldn't get changed in the studio, but we would have everything coming in.

When we finished the record, we went out on tour in the States doing twenty-five hundred- to four thousand-seaters. Things were different with the band. We were more stable and weren't worried about one of us fucking things up. It was a really good time. We also went to Europe to do some festivals and club dates.

Business-wise, things ran smoother. We were running our own management company, merchandise—everything! All the work we did on our own I'm really proud of. That's not easy to do. Before, we would get a small piece of the pie. The biggest change was that we weren't selling a million records anymore, we were selling a hundred thousand. But we were making more money than when we were selling a million records because we had turned Tesla into a cottage industry. We were being smart about how we spent our money; it was all very focused.

We were sitting at the top of this new organization, thinking we were the Beatles and Apple. But Apple went down the tubes, and we didn't want that. Once we were running the show, we found out how lucrative this business can be and how to work it to keep costs down. Making records, and the mechanics of promoting records, was fun. I enjoyed it. But doing that and managing the band while trying to be a bass player and write songs just got to be too much.

I don't think my songwriting suffered, but when you do anything in this business, it takes something out of you. You don't come out unscathed, whether you become a drug addict, or get an autoimmune disease, manic-depressive, whatever. It's not a stress-free environment, and I had a lot on my plate. I was also producing this young band, Built by Stereo, and I still had Soulmotor responsibilities.

THE PROCESSES OF RECORDING *Into the Now* and *Forever More* were similar. We rehearsed some before going into the studio but didn't have everything locked down or even completed. The big difference was having Terry Thomas producing on *Forever More*. I like different things about those two records. I think the songwriting was better on *Forever More*. Terry had something to do with that. But I think *Into the Now* is better sonically. The mix is better. It was our comeback album. It sold around two hundred fifty thousand records, so it was really important that it sold well, otherwise, there might not have been a *Forever More* or anything else.

I think Frank would say that *Into the Now* is the better record because we did it ourselves. Frank likes *Simplicity* as well, which was not on par with *Forever More* or *Into the Now*. That's not to slam Frank. He's more of an organic guy, and I'm more of a production guy. There wouldn't be a "Love Song" without Frank. I'm, frankly, more of a manufacturing guy; I have to really work at my craft. With Frank, it just flows out of him.

The title for *Into the Now* came from one of the songs. It wasn't a big statement that Tesla was back or anything. That was a coincidence. But Frank and I used to joke that the skeletons in the grave on the cover of *Forever More* were us. That's how we'd be buried when it came time.

OUR LAWYER, SHAWNA HILLEARY, called one day in 2008 and said Universal wanted to put out a Greatest Hits album. They have a series of those called *Gold*. I asked if it was in the contract that Universal had inherited when they bought Geffen some years before, and she said, "No, you don't have to give it to them."

I asked, "Why should we?" But it was kind of like an anthology and covered a lot more than *Time's Makin' Changes*. So we decided OK, we'd give it to them. They'd done this *Millennium* collection already, which was a ten-song, pretty-as-tits disc that did two hundred thousand copies. *Millennium* was just a shorter version of *Time's Makin' Changes*.

We didn't have to do this third one, but I figured they've got the catalog, and there's all this cool stuff like "Ain't Superstitious" and "The Ocean," which weren't on any Greatest Hits album. *Gold* would include some *Into the Now* songs. *Gold* seemed like it could be a great compilation album. We were involved in picking the tracks, Ross Halfin did all the photos, and it was a double album. But Universal fuckin' didn't do anything, didn't market it, or provide any support. I don't know if that's typical for that series, but we shouldn't have done it. We got kind of fucked on that. We got our mechanical royalties and stuff at least. We thought we could have done a better job with Tesla *Gold* on our own label.

There was a three-CD set called *Power Surge* that Geffen put out in 1987 after the first album that was all hard rock stuff. Whitesnake, Guns N' Roses, Sammy Hagar, and Y&T were on it. It was basically a compilation of all the rock bands on Geffen. We had four tracks on that! That was kind of interesting being packaged with those veteran bands. It was the first time seeing our material with somebody else's like, "Tesla is as good as these guys." It was a radio promotion release only, but you can find it on eBay.

Geffen released *Power Surge 2* in 1989. We had three tracks on that one, including "Rock the Nation." Geffen was great back in the day. They were the biggest, baddest fuckin' label on the planet. They drilled everything home, even *Bust a Nut*, even though it only did seven hundred thousand copies. To be able to do that at the height of the grunge movement is pretty amazing.

During the *Forever More* tour I sat down with Frank and said, "We should record a live concert and put out a DVD," as we hadn't done one since *Five Man Acoustical Jam*. I got hold of the Record Plant mobile truck, and we filmed a show in Minneapolis. Unfortunately, it was the middle of winter, and Jeff had a bad cold. But the video, *Comin' Atcha Live 2008*, was really well done and sounded really good. The only bummer was that Jeff's voice had a little bit of raspiness to it. On the newer songs, there was a growlier, gruffer sort of tone that fit in with the new material. It was more contemporary. It wasn't about how high his range was. We ended up selling almost thirty-five thousand DVDs, and all we did on the *Acoustical Jam* DVD was like twenty thousand. So we outsold what Geffen had sold on the biggest album of our career!

Throughout 2008 I managed to lose some weight—not back down to the '80s–'90s years, but enough that it was noticeable. In 2009 the stress started getting to me again, and I had another bout of colitis, this time severe enough that I had to miss two shows in the Midwest—the only two I've ever missed because of my illness. I called up one of my Sacramento homeys, Dan McNay, to fill in for me on short notice. Thanks, Dan! There were days when it was too painful to move around, and I would lay in my bunk in the bus until it was time to play. I'd go out and rock like there was nothing wrong and then go fall back into my bunk and try to sleep away the pain. Honestly, I've never been a woe-is-me kind of guy. I'm not into self-pity, in myself or others. We all have our crosses to bear, and this health thing just happens to be mine. I'm a fighter, and I'm about winning. Autoimmune disorder is my opponent. Fuck him.

It's not that easy, of course. Pain is pain, and it's a motherfucker when it's deep inside you like colitis. I get depressed sometimes, but that's different than self-pity. One thing the depression comes from is not being able to work the way I like to. It's hard to concentrate sometimes on the task at hand, whether it's onstage or in the studio. Even traveling on the bus can kick my ass. Sometimes I'll take a drink to try and kill the pain, but now I get monumental hangovers that can last a day or two, almost like a migraine. I've spoken to a lot of different people about depression, many of them doctors. I think the world today fuels the depression crisis that's going on not just in our country but all of the world. Just too many pressures, many of them brought on by social media. We know that depression can come in many different shapes and forms, so it's important to monitor your behavior. Persistent sadness that lasts for several weeks is a telltale sign of depression. Losing interest in your favorite things. Finding no fun or enjoyment in life. Losing self-confidence. They are all indicators. For me, it involves increased feelings of anxiety, wanting to go to sleep and never wake up again, and feeling empty, useless, or unable to cope with life. If and when you start to feel any of those things, it's really important to reach out and talk to somebody.

Because I have this autoimmune problem, I'm predisposed to cancers that effect the digestive system. I have to have a colonoscopy every eighteen months. But I never feel sorry for myself. It's just the price I'm supposed to pay for this great life and career.

The DVD and shows pretty much took up the next two years, and then we decided in 2011 it was time to feed the fans something new. We had these acoustic sessions that we did with Skeoch and Zutaut in 2005. They were originally supposed to be a part of a boxed set with all these unreleased demos, live tracks, videos, and stuff. It was going to be three audio CDs and two DVDs. We wanted to release it on our twenty-fifth anniversary. The problem was that we wanted to do it on our label with our promotion team, and Universal wanted to do it on theirs. We weren't going to let them fuck up our boxed set like they'd fucked up Tesla *Gold*, so we argued with them about who was going to release it, and it halted the project. I think one day we'll come to some kind of mutual agreement.

At that point in time Universal didn't own the part of the compilation that Tommy Skeoch was on. They only owned material until we broke up in '95. So in 2011 we decided to take the recordings of those acoustic sessions with Skeoch plus a couple of covers, acoustic versions, and two new tracks and build the album *Twisted Wires*. We didn't go full tilt on it like it was a brand new record. I thought people would be interested in hearing the last things Skeoch did with us, and they weren't! It didn't do very well.

Forever More, Real to Reel, and the DVD were all winners on our own label. *Twisted Wires* was the first release that did not meet the expectations of the band and distributors. Not everything you do is successful, but it has its place; it fits in the grand scheme of things and has a purpose. It's the truth. There's a great song called "2nd Street," and the first thing we did when we got back together, "I Love You," by the Climax Blues Band, the song we had recorded for Jeff's wedding. At the time I felt we should have been working on a new record, as it had been almost three years, but Jeff had just had his first child, a son, and was tied up with that. *Twisted Wires* gave us some breathing room. It was also the twentieth anniversary of *Five Man Acoustical Jam*, so we were doing acoustic shows, and *Twisted Wires* fit right into that.

Now it was time to do a new studio album from the ground up. Jeff and Frank wanted to try a different approach. Tom Zutaut said, "Let's go back and make a record like 1986." He said we could stay at his farm in Virginia, live and write together just like old times. There would be no distractions. So we did that. Then we went into a warehouse and rehearsed it all, just like we'd done with *Mechanical Resonance*. We wrote some good stuff, but making the record sound like it was 1986 was a bad call. I was outvoted. I hated it. It was a miserable experience. You can't go back in time. Make a record like Tesla 2013 is what we should have done, but Tom's like, "No," and he was wrong. There's some really good performances, but, in my opinion, it should have been approached differently. There were sloppy performances, too, and sonically it was just flat.

I thought it was going to be more of a raw approach but with modern production techniques. Instead we went with a *Real to Reel* kind of approach, but not as good. Because these were new, original songs, the performances were under the microscope. On *Real to Reel* they were classic songs we were covering. My big problem with it was Tom wasn't that much of a song guy, so I think there were half-finished things on there. I would have loved to do those songs with Phil Collen and really bring them to their full potential. But it was an experiment; we did it, some people liked it, some people, like me, didn't. It is what it is. It's history now.

On our next headline tour we opened up with "MP3" off of *Simplicity*, but on the Def Leppard tour we were doing our hits. The truth of the matter is when we go out and play these summer gigs with Leppard and Poison, or Leppard and REO, or Leppard and Styx, those people want to hear the hits. Our catalog's too deep. They're not there to hear tracks they've never heard. They want to hear familiar songs. They want to reminisce. I play to the masses, I don't play to the few, I want them all. That's probably where Frank and I butt heads sometimes, because he thinks that because fifty people on the website say they want to hear an obscure song, we should play it for them when there's ten thousand people in the audience. Well, the other 9,950 want to hear the hits, that's the majority, and I go with the majority. Always. Call me a pussy, I don't care, it's my book.

Darin's Got the Soul, I Got the Motor

I've been doing Soulmotor since the day Tesla first broke up in 1995; it's never stopped. It's just that Darin has got his movies, and I've got Tesla, so we work in between our busy schedules.

I found myself in conflict between Soulmotor and Tesla when writing songs. There's one song called "Scene of the Crime" that I presented to Tesla. They didn't want to do it. It didn't suit Jeff. I wrote it thinking it could be a Tesla song, even though most stuff I write for Soulmotor I would never consider presenting to them, knowing how Darin approaches songs. Darin and Jeff are polar opposites—equally as great though, both great fuckin' singers with their very own styles. I'm fortunate to work with two singers that I really just fuckin' love. I presented "Scene of the Crime" to Tesla and Tom liked it, and the band liked it. Jeff thought it reminded him too much of "Let Me Roll It" by Paul McCartney, so he never gravitated towards it, and I gave it to Darin. He took to it like a fish in the water. It sounds more like a Darin song; it has this Perry

Mason kind of theme to it, but I thought it would have worked as a Tesla song. On *Simplicity* I wrote "Life Is a River," which was totally for Jeff, a "Maybe I'm Amazed" kind of thing or "Let it Be," which I think is the most beautiful song ever written.

Lyrically, Tesla's darkest song is probably "Heaven's Trail," but even that's kind of uplifting. Jeff will tell you he's not religious, doesn't believe in God, but he'll write a lyric like there's no way out of this living hell unless you walk heaven's trail. I get it, even though I think it's a little bit dark, I get it as a positive because it's like saying we're fucked, but there is a way out of this. I've never really analyzed our songs that much. Jeff is almost constantly writing lyrics that look at the very best side of things. He writes hopeful songs to give people hope. He's an optimist. Over the course of time, I think that's the stuff that sticks around. People don't want to be on a bummer. None of us want to be a fuckin' bummer.

After wrapping the album, I went out on tour, and Darin made his latest movie, *Badass Monster Killer*. *Planet of the Vampire Women* was his first movie, and that was when we did the Soulmotor album *Wrong Place at the Right Time*. He was making that, and we started writing this new album while he was writing and filming that. He was busy, and I would go away on Tesla tours, and I'd write some stuff and feed it to him, so this is an accumulation of two and a half years of work that he and I were doing, and now I'm finally able to finish it. It's been sitting around for probably six, seven months, but I haven't had the time to mix. He's been busy with another film. We talked about putting this out in the near future and doing six weeks of dates behind it through the Midwest and somewhere down in Texas.

The mixes I've been doing are a lot more focused, not what was typical of Soulmotor in the past. As I said before, I started this album with just me and Darin; there was no guitar player. After *Wrong Place at the Right Time*, Mike Mathis and Dave Watts recorded some tracks, we did a few shows, and that didn't really work out with them playing live. I got this guy, Tom Armstrong-Leavitt, to play, and we got Dave Buckner, the drummer from Papa Roach, to play with us for a couple of shows. Then we got this guy, Kelly Smith, to come in because Buckner didn't work out. He's a nice guy and a great drummer, but he had a young son, so he didn't have the time. I put together a Soulmotor touring band with Tom Armstrong-Leavitt and Kelly Smith and started doing dates to support *Wrong Place at the Right Time*.

The new guys wanted to get in and write some new music, and I tried, but it's just that Darin and I work really well together. Tom Armstrong-Leavitt wanted to write, but it didn't work. He's a great player, and I like him a lot, but it was like, "I can't write songs with you." He was always the main guy in his Sacramento bands, Wynch and Hurt, but Soulmotor is me and Darin. We wrote songs with Tommy McClendon, and he was part of that sound, but Tommy was gone. That was magic; the three of us could work together.

Darin doesn't write music, just lyrics and melodies. When he starts and I give him a piece of music, he'll just go *la, la, la, blah, blah, blah, la la la la*. He won't even sing lyrics. I call it Darin language—"baaheewahey"—he just sings this melody, then we have that song, and it's like, "OK, cool, let's have some lyrics here that mean something." Then he comes back with his little mini-movies. Every song's a little mini-movie. It's always a story. That's his thing. He's not going to write a love song: "Baby I love you, Baby I'm a need you." With the internet and all, maybe he should have a mini-doc song.

Tom Armstrong-Leavitt didn't pan out, so then I got disenchanted with that, and I said to Darin, "Look, this is just hard work. I'm just going to go into my studio with my drum program, see what I come up with, then I'll start writing this stuff." He immediately gravitated to it, and we started doing it, so maybe it's a bit more commercial because it's just me writing the music. I have a commercial sensibility, and I didn't have to deal with a guitar player, because I never like the, "Well, what about my solo?" vibe. For me it's the song, it's the melody, it's the vocal. It's not about the guitar part, it's always been about the song. I've always known that, but I never had been in total control because I'm with the team. So on this record I'm a little like George Martin. It was definitely, "I'm going to write these songs. It's going to be about Darin's vocals, and the story and the music as support."

When I had killer guitar players, they wanted to be all fuckin' killer. One of the things Tommy McClendon said when he left Soulmotor was that he was leaving because he couldn't "shred." I was like, "OK, well, shred on, brother." He and I were cool, I love him, he's one of my oldest, dearest friends. There was a time after he left Soulmotor where we didn't talk, but today we are tight as we used to be, and I think we'll even work together again someday.

I play guitar kind of like a caveman, but good enough to write songs, so I just started doing demos. If you can play block chords, you can write songs. Kurt Cobain proved that to some degree, right? So that's what I started doing. Then I got Dave Rude on the record and I said, "Look, I'm playing this, this is my idea, now let's make it better." Some things he played like I played 'em, some things he played a little bit different, but it was all written by me. I enjoyed the process.

The first thing I brought Dave in on was this song called "Dream Reanimation Machine," and he immediately wrote the middle eight. He's like, "I got this idea for a bridge," and I said, "That's perfect," because Dave has real good song sensibilities; he's not just thinking about shredding all the time.

In general, some of the tracks are just me on guitar with Frank playing some solos. Some of the tracks are just Dave on guitar, cleaning up my original tracks. With riff-based songs like these, you get lots more flexibility as to who does what. Fuck it, I've been doing this a long time, I know what Soulmotor is. It's not going to happen with Tesla. Tesla's a big committee, and it's always going to be a big committee. With Soulmotor, we can be more loose, flexible, and spontaneous.

A Cottage Kind of Thing

In 2016 Tesla signed a management deal with Howard Kaufman, who was managing Aerosmith, Stevie Nicks, and Def Leppard, among others. Our main guy at the company was Mike Kobayashi. Howard was like the godfather. Unfortunately, Howard passed away in 2017, so after that, Mike took over full command of our management.

Tesla has been touring heavily since 2015, doing summer tours with Def Leppard for three years straight now. Phil Collen brought us a song that he'd written called "Save That Goodness." He also suggested that because it's the thirtieth anniversary of *Mechanical Resonance* that we record a live version of that album. So we did that and put "Save That Goodness" on as a bonus track.

The band liked the production that Phil did on "Save That Goodness" so much that we asked him to produce our next studio album. We recorded tracks out on the road. Phil might say, "Let's do that solo today." So after sound check, Phil, Frank, and I would go into a recording room I have set up at all shows and lay it down. It's a great way to work.

Tesla wouldn't be where we are if it weren't for Def Leppard, straight up. They've always been supportive of us. They're our big brothers. They must like us. Ever since they gave us those little four-track tape decks, they've always looked out for us. Phil was telling us now, "You need to dress better onstage." So during a tour break we got a few wardrobe people to come up to Sacramento where we were shooting the "Save That Goodness" video. You can see the difference. No more T-shirts and ripped jeans. It looks great onstage as well.

My health got a lot better around then too. Just staying out of stressful situations is key. Really, it's just how I react to stress. Diet is the other thing. When I had raw chef Jeni Cook preparing all my meals, it was wonderful. But it's not practical on the road. We don't get enough room for her to set up everything she needs. Eating raw is very involved, more intense than vegetarian and vegan, because nothing is cooked. Getting the full benefit of the nutrients in the raw food is what really controls the inflammation caused by the autoimmune disease. I had Jeni come out to my home for three months during our six-month break in 2018, alternating months. I went all-out on the raw food and got ready for the back end of 2018, when we were on the road the whole time.

My goal for my weight is 170 pounds. I'll never get back to 150, that's unreasonable. I think it would actually be unhealthy to do what I'd have to do to lose that much weight. But 170 is attainable. I'm under 200 pounds now, but it gets tougher as I lose the core weight that I've been at for decades now. The prednisone weight actually comes off pretty easy as long as I stay on the regimen of exercise and diet. This last 25 pounds is gonna be a bitch, but that won't stop me.

In November 2015 something happened that is pretty much the highlight of my career, if not my entire life. Jimmy Page was being honored in Seattle at the EMP Museum. Many rock luminaries performed his music for him that night: Rick Nielsen from Cheap Trick, Duff McKagan from Guns N' Roses, along with guys from Soundgarden, Alice in Chains, Nirvana, and others—and me, of all people. Given my friendship with Jimmy, I was asked to be there and play with Jimmy's one-time The Firm bandmate Paul Rodgers, which was a thrill in itself because I'm a huge fan of Paul's going all the way back to Free and Bad Company.

I get up to play on stage with Paul, and when Jimmy sees me from his seat, he just smiles and starts laughing like he can't believe it. He didn't know I was going to be there, and I guess he was pleasantly surprised. We are making lots of eye contact and sharing the inside joke as friends, which was already a pretty fucking cool thing. But then the bar gets raised. I don't think anybody ever expected Jimmy to really get up and play, but, just in case, there was a Les Paul on stage with his name on it. As the tribute is wrapping up, Jimmy comes up on stage to huddle up, and it appears as if it is "game on." Now it's getting interesting. He straps on the Les, leans over to me as we are standing in front of the drums, and whispers the question, "What are we going to do?" Well, I mean what else would we do? Zeppelin's "Rock and Roll!" He nods and then his expression changes. It's game time. Fire's in his eyes and all that. He's becoming Jimmy fucking Page right before my eyes as he counts in the song and then *boom*, there are those cords that came screaming out of my speakers when I was a kid. And I'm right next to him playing bass as the band rips through one of the all-time Zeppelin classics. If that was my last night on the planet I would've left with a huge smile on my face. I was floating on air.... Talk about a dream come true—playing next to my pal Jimmy Page onstage. I woke up the next morning thinking it had been a dream, but there on the homepage of Rolling Stone was a picture of the event, two shots featuring me and Jimmy, playing next to each other. Thinking about it now, yeah, this was definitely the highlight of my life.

Tesla has definitely become a brand. We've built it into that. Recording and touring is what makes it work. We can go another ten years, I think. But we need to put out records that will build a new audience. If we can't do that, I don't know how long I'll keep going. We're at a level now that is tough for me because of my health. I need a full-size bed in the back lounge of a bus, and I need to control my diet. We're not making the kind of money that will let me do that. We need to go up a level in terms of our draw. Then I could do that. But I'm a team player. I started this thing with Frank, and I'm all in for as long as I can.

I'm in a position today where I'm really the only guy in the band who can handle all the shit that happens. Whether it's Jeff or Troy, sometimes even Frank, I'm the only guy who handles those situations. There are no surprises. Mike is great as a manager, but he hasn't got those years of influence, of credibility with the guys. Our road manager doesn't have that either. Sometimes it's push coming to shove, and it's me. Just is. Sometimes I don't want it, but I have it.

You've already gotten the sense that I can be a little rough around the edges, and I'm aware of that. It's part of my personality. Sometimes in meet-and-greets, if we're having a business problem or internal band spat, I can be a little gruff with the fans. Jeff, Frank, and Dave are always real nice with the fans, but I've got a rep as being a little antisocial on occasion. My autoimmune issues can set me on edge as well. I've only missed three shows in thirty-five years, and they were all because I couldn't stand up or even get out of bed. So, I'll be the asshole, but I'm the asshole who's kept the band together. Sorry fans, nothing personal.

I don't think a breakup is imminent. There's still frustration in the band. There's four guys who have very strong opinions and don't always agree, but we always find a way where majority rules. It scared the shit out of me when I got sick on a recent tour. I thought maybe I should stay at home, take some time off, and let someone else go out there and play while I try to get healthy. I've got everything under control, and it feels good to be back out with the band again. I don't like touring, but I love playing. When we're out there on stage it feels great, no one can get to us. But being on a bus with twelve people and having to compromise to other peoples' schedules and all that shit takes its toll. I've got to find a place today where it's not too taxing on my health, and I'm starting to do that.

I try to not think about the next attack, which almost surely will happen someday. That would just increase my stress and make the next onset come sooner and bigger. It's so hard to do. The pressures that cause the stress aren't going away. There are very few issues I confront and decisions I make or am involved in that are unimportant. Most of them have a significant effect on both Tesla and Soulmotor in some way. There are almost always financial considerations and fallout that have to be dealt with, and much of all that can be unpredictable and complicated. The music business is nothing if not flaky because at heart, it's about people's taste, and that's subjective. Whether it's the band, the fans, the larger audience, or the suits that run the corporations, no one can predict what's next. That's why everyone tends to jump on the new fad, because as the saying goes, nothing succeeds like success.

In the Captain's Chair

The first thing I ever worked on as a producer was a 58 Fury demo that I did with Frank in 1988.

I used to go to Oasis on Sunday nights, which showcased new artists, looking for talent. So 58 Fury was there one night doing all this old stuff like Faces and the Stones, and all this cool rhythm and blues music. They did a great version of "Heartbreaker." I thought, *Wow, that's really cool, they're going back to the '70s.* It was the stuff I grew up on, not Ratt or Mötley Crüe, which is what most cover bands were playing. The band was Ned, Chris, Virgil, Brett, and Darin Wood. The drummer was a guy I nicknamed "Scrumble Bum." I started hanging out with them. I remember giving them Humble Pie tapes, turning them on to stuff I thought they'd like but didn't know about. I thought Darin was a super cool dude. We hit it off. I got real close to Virgil as well.

I invited the band to make some tapes. I wasn't that confident on my own, so I asked Frank to help, and we produced it together. The gear we used belonged to Waylin Carpenter from Steel Breeze, and we worked at Harbor Studios in West Sacramento. That was

John Wiseman and George Gosling's place. I gave the demo to Steve Clausman and he loved it. He loved old R&B: Little Feat and all that stuff. Steve got them a deal. They never made a record because they fucked it all up, but that's where Darin and I developed our friendship. A few years back they got back together and did a few shows, and when Tesla played Thunder Valley, I had them open up. Because they were from South Sac and I felt this kinship to them, I wanted them to play a really big show. They kicked ass.

I started producing on my own when Tesla broke up, and I created Soulmotor. That was out of necessity. I got some gear and started recording in my house. Dan McClendon used to engineer and help me. I just gravitated towards it and started to dig it. I still enjoy it. It's like a drug addiction. Once you get into it, you start buying all this equipment. You go crazy with it.

I built a little studio in my bedroom, but outgrew the space, so I built a proper studio at the back of my house. On one of the drives that Tesla was making from Sacramento to the Midwest to start a tour, I was sitting in the back of the lounge with my bass tech, Marco Bustos. A talented guy, he was also a general contractor. He said he could help me build it, so we drew up plans on the back of a napkin. I had been in enough recording studios to have a working sense of basic design.

He built houses, and I'd been in a lot of studios, so we just started researching and designing. This was going to be a two-story building out in back of my house. The lots downtown are really deep with an alley along the back. I had a garage on the bottom facing the alley, then a small kitchen, lounge, and office. I had another room that was originally a small satellite control room, but I converted that into a bunkroom with six beds, so I could have bands from out of town stay at the studio.

The studio took up the entire upstairs. Just about half of the upstairs were the recording spaces, and half was the control room. I knew I was going to have to get a Neve console, and I found one that was owned by Dominic Frontiere, who did orchestral arrangements on the Tubes' first album and the '60s TV show *The Outer Limits*. He also did the music for Clint Eastwood's movie *Hang 'Em High*. We mixed *Into the Now* there, recorded *Forever More* there, and half of *Real to Reel*.

I took Built by Stereo through the whole process of learning to write songs and recording. Lots of people came and worked there including Papa Roach, Pat Travers, and the Deftones.

While I was mastering the Soulmotor and Built by Stereo albums in New York, my life changed. I was using one of the top mastering engineers, George Marino, and both of these sessions were on my dime, so I wasn't staying at the Four Seasons. My bed was in a little shitbag hotel in Chinatown. I had Tesla's road manager, Jimmy Dean, with me in the double occupancy room. That's what a cheap bastard I can be.

As John Lennon said, "Life is what happens when you're busy making plans." That's about as true as it gets. The second day in the mastering lab, my wife called. She was very upset that our cat had brought in a mauled squirrel, and she didn't want to deal with it. She didn't know if it was dead or alive. I called Marco to go over to the house and get rid of the little rodent. After finishing the session around six in the evening, Jimmy Dean and I grabbed some dinner before heading back to the shitbag to turn in early. Tesla was beginning a short run of shows in Michigan, and we were on an early flight out in the morning. It was around four in the morning when the phone rang. Only my wife would call me at that time, and only if something was seriously wrong. Sure enough the screen on my iPhone read "Monique." In my waking-up fog I could only imagine it was another zombie rodent issue. It was one in the morning in Sacramento. What the hell?

Pressing the Answer button, all I heard was Monique scream-ing incoherently. I couldn't make out what she was saying. I was trying to get her to calm down when I heard sirens in the back-ground, quiet at first, but getting louder by the second. Monique was freaking out; she didn't know what to do. "Fire!" I finally heard her yelling. "Fire!"

I said, "Take the fuckin' dogs and get out of the fuckin' house. We got insurance!" What the fuck? Was this really happening? First and foremost, obviously, were Monique and the dogs. They were going to be OK. But my Victorian house and studio—was I about to lose everything? I was three thousand miles away, and I felt con-fused and helpless. Talk about an anxiety trigger.

I gathered my thoughts and did what, in all the chaos, seemed like the most sensible thing. I called back and spoke with one of the firemen. "Look, it's a recording studio; try to get everything you can out of there, my guitars and stuff, but especially the hard drives." And they did. They saved tons of shit. They tried to save the console. It could be fixed, but it would be more to fix it than to buy another.

I asked him, "Is my house in danger?" I said, "Whatever you do, don't let my house burn down."

And he said, "Well there's embers flying onto your roof and your roof is wood shake, which is dangerous." I said just keep water on it. So there was water damage in my house. They blew the roof off. Those water hoses, they doused it. Water went straight into my attic and came down. But still, they did the best they could, and I was thankful.

Jimmy got us both the first flight back to Sacramento, and we raced over to the scene. They were able to save the house, but the studio was a complete loss. Most of the gear was completely fuckin' ruined. Some of my guitars were OK, some of them were more fucked up. The insurance company wouldn't pay me on my guitars; I fought with them for two years, and they wouldn't pay. I said they were my personal property. No, no, they said they weren't my personal property, they were business property. They said because I played music they were all in the studio, and I'm like, "No, they're mine. So you're saying if I'm a race car driver, and I have a race car, every other car I have aren't my personal cars but are the race car company's?" They waited me out and won; good old State Farm Insurance, any insurance, they just try to fuckin' grind you down. I beat 'em up, I got a lot of money out of 'em, they just wouldn't pay for my guitars. They paid for two of them, then they said fuck, we're not paying for any other ones. They paid for the Hofner, and I still got it and it's all right. I was able to get it restored, and I had a few extra bucks left over. People were hearing about the fire around town; people were coming over, and it was on the news. "The rock band Tesla's studio burned down," not Brian Wheat's studio, but whatever, I didn't care.

This guy, Mike Brown, was holding court, talking to all the news people like he was our press agent, "Well this is going to set the band back." The whole thing was surreal; this dude's holding court with the fuckin' news people in Sacramento, my wife's freaking out. When she left, she ran across the street. Out of everything in the house she grabbed a pair of sunglasses and two pairs of jeans and ran out with the dogs. At least she got the dogs.

I was numb. It was just like I was in a trance. I walked in there and saw all this devastation...*fuuuccckkkk*. I was almost paralyzed; I didn't know what to do. I wasn't crying or freaking out, I was just like blown away, what in the fuck? You don't know what being displaced feels like until you have a fire like that. All my stuff, everything that was in my house, in my studio, on the property, went to this big warehouse in West Sacramento, and it was under lockdown. The insurance company took this entire inventory, and they were assessing what was and wasn't damaged.

They never thought it was arson, or I did it, or anything. The insurance company just didn't want to pay on anything. I remember meeting the adjuster, and all my guitars were there. They all smelled like smoke, some of the necks were fucked up. And he said, "These are a complete loss, total loss." I said OK. Waited two years, and they didn't cover them. One thing I gotta say is if you have a fire, hire an independent adjuster, don't use the insurance company's adjuster. I had this guy, Richard Csaposs, who found all kinds of stuff in my policy for me. He was worth every penny I paid him.

I wasn't able to get in my house right away; I had to go play. I'd missed another gig. I called a local bass player, Dan McNay, and said "Look, can you go cover for me?"

He said, "I can only do one show, Brian."

I'm like, "OK, I'll take whatever you can give me," so he went and did it. Jimmy took off and met the band, and I flew out the next day. Dan knew my stuff because he had filled in for me when I got sick with colitis. That's the three shows I missed: one for the fire and two for my autoimmune disease.

The insurance company rented us a loft down at J Street, and we stayed in there with Bonnie and Clyde for about six months. Then they rebuilt the house, and then it was like, well, what do I do with this back building where the studio was? I remember Troy telling me, "One day you'll look back on this, and you'll think it's OK." I didn't know what he meant at the time, but now I know. I was better off after the fire in a lot of ways. I got to build the studio properly, this time with a designer. I got to do it at a different location. My first studio had a lot of drawbacks. It was in my backyard, it was on the second floor, and people who would just be visiting me were still at my house—too close to my personal stuff.

What I liked about it was I could go from my house into my backyard to work in the studio. Monique was thirty feet away. If there was a problem I'd come running in; fifteen seconds and I'd be in the house. Now when I go to the studio it's ten blocks away, so I come home by one o' clock in the morning; I don't stay there until six, seven in the morning like I used to.

I didn't get my stuff back for a year. I had to assess what was salvageable. They wrote a lot of it off. Tesla recorded *Twisted Wires* during that time. We recorded some stuff at Frank's place and then we mixed it at Sonic Ranch. That fire was in 2010, and we're sitting here talking about it in 2020, and I still got half of a three-thousand-square-foot warehouse full of shit from that fire that hasn't been gone through. Some of it's good, some of it's shit that needs to go to the dump. Some of it's been on my new engineer Jack's plate. We still got the Neve console. We're going to salvage parts off it. There's just tons of stuff. What do I do with all this shit?

One simple thing caused all this. Somebody was barbecuing in the apartment house next door. No one got hurt, that was the main thing, and that's what I told Monique—this shit's all replaceable. But it was very depressing. It was like a death; you've put so much time and effort into it. Until I got the new studio up and running, I couldn't produce anything or anyone. That took three years. I didn't have a portable rig then like I have now. The technology wasn't practical in 2010.

Once I got over the shock and was able to think clearly, the fire actually gave me the chance to correct a lot of things that weren't right with the studio. I knew that I wasn't going to rebuild the studio in back of my house. That was a big thing. It was going to be on the ground floor. That was another big thing. And then there were a whole lot of things to do with the electrical and the acoustics, the way the recording room and the control room were arranged, the materials in the walls and ceiling. The new studio has a clamshell over the Neve. That is an acoustic diffuser that keeps sound from echoing off the ceiling.

When Marco and I first looked at the building where the studio is now, I didn't think it would be big enough. The place had been a photo lab, so it was divided up into offices and a few bigger rooms where they had the developing tanks and printers and stuff. Marco then suggested that I buy a warehouse, and we'd build the whole studio as a building inside the warehouse. He said it could be modular, so if I ever wanted to move it, it would come apart and could be moved to another warehouse. That's some Magic Alex stuff there!

I leased a 3,500-square-foot warehouse in an industrial area of Sacramento. Half of it was for Tesla's equipment, and the other half was for the studio. We started building the studio using all steel framing. I was using insurance money from the fire, and I put about $10,000 into this steel framing. It was looking kind of hokey, and I started having doubts whether I wanted to even have another studio. We talked about building a portable rig, just a control room that could be moved, but that didn't go far.

I found a piece of land, an empty lot downtown that was at the end of a street right next to a new housing development. It was zoned commercial, so I called Brian Clausman. Brian had been into real estate for many years at that point, and we agreed to look into building the studio there as well as practice facilities and maybe even a music store and other stuff, a whole complex. Marco was still into the first building, the ex-photo lab. He kept telling me it was big enough, that he could make it work. I went and looked at the building again, and this time I could see what Marco was saying, how it could work. So I switched gears and committed to the photo lab.

Brian and I then decided that we'd put condos up on the empty lot. I couldn't do both at the same time, so Brian loaned me $400,000 to get the studio going. We ran into a snag on the condo lot, because we needed to get an easement from the business next door to tap into their sewer line. Otherwise, we would have to run our own line all the way down the street, maybe a half-million dollars' worth. The dude didn't want to do it, so that project stalled out, and we just sat on the empty lot.

The owner of the photo lab building had a run-down bungalow right next door, and he would only sell them together. He suggested I tear down the house and use the area for studio parking. In the meantime, I had rebuilt the building in back of my house as a detached extension of the house but using the same paint and construction materials. I had to go around and around with the insurance company on all the destroyed contents of the studio, but they had paid right away on the burned building itself.

The Victorian house had a small kitchen. In 1896 when the house was built, kitchens were not the social centers they are now. So on the ground floor of the back building—I called it the Barn—I built a proper kitchen and a bedroom. On the front half of the second floor I had a theater/media room/man cave and, in the back, a gym and also a sewing room for Monique. So I had a bit of a renovation bug, and I wanted to fix that bungalow up. But the studio had to come first.

I hired Vincent Van Hoff to design the rooms. Marco and I had done the designs ourselves on the old studio. But room tuning and acoustics are very important in a studio, otherwise, you can't trust what you're hearing. So I learned from that and hired a professional to design the new studio. It turned out to be one of the last designs Vincent did, as he passed away soon after.

The first studio always had weird little electrical gremlins, being on the old downtown electrical grid, and we didn't do a great job on the grounding; we didn't isolate the circuits as well as we might have. We straightened all of that out in the new place.

Because I was planning on producing other bands, most of whom would be from out of town, I built three bedrooms, each with two beds, and a kitchen and dining area. Just recently though, my new house engineer, Jack, had some ideas about how to put those rooms to better use, so we converted them into a couple of mixing rooms and a storage room for mics and other gear.

Once the new studio was up and running, I didn't have a lot of time to do other projects because Tesla was taking up most of my time. I went through several guys as producer/engineers who didn't work out, and then finally one guy ripped me off. While I was out on tour, some amps, mics, and other gear went missing from the studio. When I got back I couldn't get hold of him. It turns out the gear had been hocked. I changed the locks on the building to keep him out. I should have had him arrested.

The very day that happened I found this great guy, Jack O'Donnell, to run the studio. He came in to see me and brought a condenser microphone he had built. That was impressive. He had great ideas for the studio, he's mellow and creative, and he wanted to rehab a lot of the damaged gear from the old studio. So I brought him on, and he became the house producer, engineer, and marketing guy. He still does it all. When we were in doing *Shock* with Phil producing, the engineer we were using couldn't make it in one day. Jack just took over and never let go. He finished the album. I just want to keep the studio busy, and Jack is doing just that. You don't really make a lot running a recording studio, but I own the building and the gear, so that's where the value is.

The trick of the recording art today is knowing when a song or album is finished and then leaving it alone. I'm not a fan of vocal auto-tuning, which is very popular. You need to be able to sing in tune, otherwise, what's the point? Anyone could do it, but it sounds unnatural. I had a girl in singing on a session, and she wasn't hitting notes. I wanted her to redo those areas, and she said, "You can just auto-tune them." When I told her that I don't do that, she started crying. She got butthurt. Not everyone is cut out for this business.

I do grid drums a lot. That means that I manipulate the drum performance for the rest of the band to track to so that the performance is absolutely in time. There is just no room for even the smallest unintentional drift in meter. Otherwise, the bass is always trying to lock to something that's off. You can't have that. Records today are sonically huge, and the smallest shift in those fundamental things really stands out against the competition. On the other hand, I don't ever grid guitars. I like to let them sway if it makes for a good feel. The same with vocals.

That's today's market. That's just the way it is. And that's why I'm not thrilled with *Simplicity*. The band was dead set against gridding the drums. I think the sessions for *Real to Reel* down in Texas got everyone thinking about going old school, but in order to compete with Kid Rock, Matchbox 20, or Train, that wasn't very realistic. It really bummed me out.

On *Forever More* we used my first studio for everything. Terry Thomas stayed at my house, and we brought back Michael Rosen to do the engineering. Michael had a great feel for the band and was easy to work with. Although one time he did get on my nerves; I'm not always as patient as maybe I should be. While I was tracking the bass, he said it sounded like I was out of tune. I said it sounded fine to me, and Terry agreed. But Michael wasn't having it, and I told him to just shut up and press the record button. I'm sorry Michael, that's just me.

There's no money to be made putting out records anymore, not for most of the bands at our level. The whole business model is backwards from before 2000. It used to be that you toured to support album sales, now you put out records to get people out to the shows. Selling merchandise at shows and through our website brings in money too. So expenses on the road are a major concern now; it can make or break a tour. We couldn't survive without income from touring.

There's a logical path that's hard to avoid for a young band that gets signed and has success. You start with no money, no real concept of what it means to have money. Then you get a lot of attention, you get fans. Now you're a celebrity to some degree. Then maybe you start getting the money. Then you pass the peak. Now you have to be smarter or else. All these things put you through changes, and your character either pulls you through, or you sink or burn out. I know; I've lived all of that.

I NEVER THOUGHT I'D LEAVE SACRAMENTO. I was born there, raised there, my family is there, my band is there. I own a beautiful Victorian house there, and my studio is there. But there are several reasons why I moved to Texas in 2017. There isn't one that is more important than the others; it's really the sum of them all.

One thing is that there is no state income tax in Texas. My tax rate in California is no more than 10 percent. That's a lot of money. Another thing is that Sacramento has developed quite a homeless problem, especially in the Midtown area where I live. I find human shit and piss around our house a lot. Our garbage is always thrown all over from them digging through the garbage cans. They even try tapping into our electrical box! Monique is scared all the time when I'm not there. She can't go out around there at night anymore.

Another thing happened back in 2012 that probably had a bit to do with my estrangement from the Sacramento house. Both Bonnie and Clyde died that year of old age; they were both fifteen years old. When Monique and I got past that, we found another brother-and-sister pair of Jack Russells, Spanky and Darla. It took a while to feel like I could accept them. Spanky and Darla weren't bred as domestically as Bonnie and Clyde, so they were kind of going stir crazy with the small yard they had to romp in.

I belong to this Victorian homeowners group on Facebook. While I was on tour in 2017 I saw this beautiful Victorian house for sale on the group. The price was $2.5 million, and I thought, *Well, I can't afford that.* But the house was beautiful. I looked at it again later, and I realized I had read the price incorrectly. It was $250,000 not $2.5 million. That got my attention! This stuff I mentioned above was going through my mind, so I called Monique and asked her if she would consider moving to Texas. She was all for it since she grew up near Dallas, and it was like going home for her.

This house, in Baird about twenty miles west of Abilene, was 5,500 square feet, about 1,500 square feet bigger than the Sacramento house. In addition, it had a detached garage with an apartment above that. It was on an acre and a half of land. Spanky and Darla were so high-strung that we couldn't even take them to a dog park, or any park. They would just go crazy, yelp, and try to fight other dogs. So this house would have a ton of space for them to run around.

The lifestyle in Sacramento was great when I was in my thirties and forties, lots of places to go drinking and party, including my house! But I'm in my fifties now, and I still spend six to eight months every year on the road. Now when I come home, I want more space, not as much noise and traffic. I only ever went about eight blocks from home in Midtown; I'm pretty much of a homebody. It's about the same in Baird, only the blocks aren't full of restaurants, bars, and clubs. I have to go about five miles to the next town, Clyde, to get some food. If I go twenty miles, I'm in Abilene, which has a population of about 120,000, so they have anything there.

It's better for my health in a number of ways. Just the general energy level of life in Midtown always got me kind of fidgety; it was tough to get into relax mode. I eat healthier in Texas because I can't just walk two blocks to get a heavy meal or fast food. I can't even get a pizza delivered!

We make our meals at home much more than we ever have. I like to cook. Anyone who's seen my Facebook page has seen pictures of me grilling up some fine food. The diet on I'm on now, called the HCG diet, has me eating more chicken and fish than beef. I dearly love a good steak, but I'm cutting back on the cow. The veggies I can eat are asparagus, broccoli, mushrooms, cucumbers, zucchini, and tomatoes.

A big help when losing weight is that your stomach shrinks so you don't eat as much to get full. You can't just gorge; you have to be sensible. Full means full. I have a weight coach, and she encourages me when I'm hungry between meals to snack on protein, like a chicken breast or grilled fish. On this program even fruits are not that good for me after the morning, so I won't even eat an apple after breakfast. From lunch on it's all veggies and then the meat for protein, but no pork or lamb and no organs, like liver or kidneys. I wouldn't eat that shit anyway. The beef is always lean like a filet mignon or flank steak. Porterhouse steaks or ribs are loaded with fat, so I won't eat those.

The only member of my family that I'm close to is my older brother, Buddy. He's seventy-one as of this writing, and we get along great. I'm trying to get him to sell his house in Sac and move out to Baird. Right now he's in the apartment above the garage, but you can get a lot of house here compared to Northern California. Buddy always looked out for me, so I want to repay him for that and have him around. I like to travel with him, and we enjoy going over to Italy when we can. Besides, I've already found him a girlfriend in Texas!

I think I've got something of a "Winchester complex." Sarah Winchester was the widow/heir of the guy who invented the Winchester rifle, which, when the American West was being settled, was the rifle that was most widely used. Sarah, who they say was a little wiggy, had this guilt complex that the family fortune came from something that killed thousands of people. She had this crazy idea that if she kept adding rooms to her house that those souls would find peace. There are 161 rooms and forty-seven fireplaces in the famous Winchester Mystery House, which is in San Jose, California. I get where she was coming from!

There are some things I want to do with the house, not that crazy though. The kitchen needs to be bigger, so that will push the exterior walls out about eight feet or so. I want to put in a pool and a well. Also a storm shelter. Then there's the whole new building for the recording studio and theater. There is one slightly crazy thing. The sky is so clear in Baird that I want to build an observatory.

I'VE DEVELOPED A REAL LOVE FOR PHOTOGRAPHY, and I've found that I'm pretty good at it. When I reconnected with Ross Halfin in 2008, I started messing around with it. Ross and I did quite a bit of traveling during the time after my studio burned down. Ross always took this little Leica camera with him wherever he went. I don't think he takes a shit without that camera. I got a Leica myself, and Ross started showing me how to use it. Then I got a Nikon, and Ross gave me a D3S. I use that bad boy mostly now. I really like shooting landscapes and architecture. Occasionally, I'll take pictures of people, but usually only in exotic places, like Thailand or Italy, where the culture is different.

I try to go to Italy three or four times a year. I've been going for fifteen years now. It's just so beautiful. It's a place where I can relax and recharge. The pace out in the country is so much slower. I don't have to be "that guy" over there. Nobody cares about that.

I started vacationing in Italy in 2005. We played Milan in 1991 with the Scorpions, but that wasn't what got me interested. One day I woke up, maybe it was 2006, and I was watching that show, *Rome*, on HBO. I got really intrigued with Italy. My family's from Italy; I saw the movie *Under the Tuscan Sun*. I just decided one day, *I want to go to Tuscany on vacation*. So Monique and I, and my brother and his girlfriend at the time went over. And when I got there I found this place that was magical to me, this villa. I knew Tuscany was the region I wanted to go to, but I didn't know that much about Italy. I got there, and it just spoke to me.

I wanted to go back, over and over and over. It was like a magnetic attraction. I could not resist, so I kept going to the same place, and I found that I would go there before a tour to gear up for the work year and then at the end to decompress. Christmas or October, always. If the touring cycle was from April to September, then we'd take off October through February. Usually in March we'd start again. I'd go decompress in October for a week. It was like my sanctuary.

I went to this villa that a family named Poro owned. Michela, Mateo, Miko, Marta, Maximo, and Maria. Maximo is a molecular scientist. He invented the vaccine for spinal meningitis; he's a pretty heavyweight dude. I guess he's pretty wealthy, so he built Michela this villa as a business to rent out. Michela and I became good friends because I kept going back. She's like a sister to me. Their family's like an adopted family to me, Monique, and Buddy. And then I was like, I need my own place. In the back of my mind I started thinking about when I slow down, I want to spend three or four months a year in Italy.

At that point I'd like to have my own house instead of going to their place, which is beautiful, and great, as they don't charge because I always bring people to fill the place up. They love me, they love me like family, and Monique and Buddy as family as well. But I just wanted to get my own place. So now we have our own villa in Tuscany, about a mile from their villa. The family lives in Scrofiano, and I live at the bottom of their village in Fontecchio, and the villa's in the village over in Rigomagno. And Michela and her brother live in Siena.

It's a peaceful place; I can go there and not have to worry about the pressures of being in Tesla or anything. People can't get to me.

They can't call and say, "I need something," because I'm fuckin' gone, nine hours ahead of everybody; you're half way around the world, and I'm able to really relax there. People live a lot slower there. At two o'clock, they take a siesta, a three-hour lunch, till five o'clock. They go home, eat, fuck, drink, sleep, whatever, and then go back to work. There's a difference between dinner and supper in Europe; you eat dinner about nine-thirty, ten o'clock. In Italy, you eat late, but the big meal is lunch.

My Winchester complex will probably follow me to Tuscany. I've already kind of maxed out the main villa, but I have another piece of land across a shared private road. Over there I will build a garage and a small guest house. I'll put a gate and fence around it, and that'll be where you park the cars. But recently I spent a year redoing this one, remodeling two bathrooms, a kitchen, a living room, putting in a bunch of sprinklers and fences and new security cameras. Surveillance man, I have to see what's going on, like Scarface.

Now the Sacramento house is fairly empty, and my primary residence is in Baird, Texas. We made the move, and I'm glad we did. I'm not going to get rid of the Victorian; my plan is to rent it for three to five years. The way it was set up, it was a single-family house. It was built in 1895 by Mr. Hill, who was a prominent buggy maker and had a lot of money. Unfortunately for him, the automobile came into common use around the turn of the century. That was the end of the buggies, and he lost a lot of his money. He divorced his wife and moved up to Loomis and started a pear farm.

Mrs. Hill stayed, she obviously kept the house, and she and her two children lived in the downstairs part. They turned the upstairs, where there were four bedrooms, into two apartments: one bedroom, living room, and a little kitchenette. Downstairs are two parlors, a dining room, a kitchen, two bedrooms, and a bathroom. So I turned it back into three apartments, like she had it, and I'm renting them out. The back house, the Barn, I'm going to turn into two Airbnb apartments. There's still stuff being stored there in the gym and the theater room. Jonathan, one of the guys who works with me, is living in the downstairs part of the Barn, he and his lady, India, and getting the upstairs ready for rental.

I was going to redo the whole basement in the Vic, which would have added eighteen hundred square feet to the J Street house, and in that basement was going to be a huge gourmet kitchen, but I bought the place in Italy instead, and there went that year's budget for Winchester disease.

Baird is nice. Our new neighbors are coming over, offering help, bringing us home-baked pies and things. No one ever did that to me in Midtown, and I lived there twenty-two years. No one ever came over and said, "Hi, I'm your next-door neighbor." So it's kind of nice, I like it. Eventually that will all settle down, and there will be a familiarity with everybody, and I'll know how much I like it here. I know, deep down in my heart, it's a good thing being here. I definitely want a quieter lifestyle when I'm not on tour, and I like having a big yard for the dogs.

Just saying "dogs" isn't easy because of what happened a few weeks after we settled into the house. Spanky and Darla were having a gas playing in their new big yard. In preparation for the move, we had gotten them vaccinated for rattlesnake venom, because in West Texas that's what you should do. One day just before Thanksgiving in 2017, a rattlesnake got in the yard, and Spanky and Darla, being natural born hunters, went after it. Darla got struck three times and died on the way to the vet. Spanky was struck once, but the snake had used most of its venom on Darla, so he survived. Monique was right there when it happened and was just devastated. I don't know if she'll ever get over it completely. Because I had to hit the road for a while after that, I felt like I needed to hide my guns. I was that worried about her. I had one of her close friends fly out for a few days to be with her. Darla and Spanky killed the snake, by the way.

Not too soon after the move to Texas, I started to experience weakness in my right hand. It looked initially like it might be my neck, something serious. Tesla was going to South America in December of 2017 for some shows with Deep Purple and Cheap Trick, and I didn't know if I could play. After several MRIs and different doctors' opinions, it turned out to be a nerve impingement in my shoulder. I had some physical therapy done and it subsided, so I was able to go.

Before I left, Monique found a Jack Russell puppy in Paris, Texas. It was going to be ready for adoption in about six weeks. We said OK, great. Then while I was in South America, Monique saw another puppy online that looked a lot like Darla. Now she wants this one as well. I'm kind of in a fog by this point. Two, three, six dogs, whatever. I just want to see my wife smile again, right? So when I get back from the tour, we drive to Dallas to see this second dog and bring her back to Baird. We named her Thelma.

As I said, for the past several years, Monique and Buddy and I always go to Italy for Christmas. This year we were going to take Spanky and Darla. We got the emotional support animal papers so they could fly with us. But now it's just Spanky, and we can't take Thelma; she's just too young. She stayed home with the housekeeper, Brandi. We were just licking our wounds, so to speak.

When we got back, we went up to Paris for the first puppy. We named her Louise. While we were there, Louise's brother came trotting out and was just the cutest little guy. This was Alfalfa. I wasn't sure if Spanky would accept a new male dog in the house. But it seems to be working out fine. Spanky lets the puppies know when he doesn't want to be bothered, but it's just a little growling, nothing physical.

In addition to the big move to Texas, I grew a lot creatively around 2017. I had been traveling all over the world both on tour and on vacation, oftentimes with Ross. Basically, I would mimic what he would be shooting, from landscapes to landmarks, and one day he said to me, "You know, you have a good eye." I told him I didn't know shit about the technical side of photography, but he continued, "That doesn't matter. You have a good eye for composition, which is a very important thing." That made me feel pretty good. Shortly after that we were on the Monsters of Rock Cruise, and I saw Rick Allen was on board selling his paintings. I'm an enterprising guy, always thinking about business, so I tracked down the head of the Wentworth Gallery, Christian O'Mahoney, who was on board helping Rick facilitate the on-ship gallery.

"Hey man," I said to him. "What are the odds you might want to take some of my photographs and create a gallery so that fans might be able to purchase them?"

He explained to me, "Look, these are really good photos that you take. But I do fine art, not photography. Sorry."

The next day he tracked me down and seemed to have had a change of heart. "I have an idea," he said. "I really like your photos. Would you consider painting on your photos?" I didn't know what the hell he was talking about.

"I'm not a painter," I said.

"Look, you don't have to be a painter, per se," he said. "You can enhance your photographs by painting right on top of them." Once we all got back home, I sent him some of my images, and he sent them back after having had them produced on a variety of services like metal and canvas. I liked the canvas best. So I started painting on top of them. Monique had taken some art classes, so she had a bunch of easels and paint. Once I sent a couple of samples back to Christian, he said "This is great. This is something I can definitely work with."

What makes the works so special is that even if I use the same photo, I never paint on the same photo the same way, so each piece of art becomes completely unique, a one-of-one. It's really like stress therapy for me. It helps to ease so much of my anxiety on the road. After you have a sound check, you've usually got four, five hours to kill. So I started going into my dressing room, burning some incense, playing some Beatles, and painting. I mostly use acrylics, because I find them more forgiving, along with paint pens, colored sharpies, and some other things. I've had a number of exhibits in galleries and on concert cruises. The first piece I ever sold was to a woman who had never even heard of Tesla, which made me feel good. I know fans like these pieces because it helps connect to them to the band. But I've also had a lot of people who know nothing about rock 'n' roll come up to me and say they like the art for what it is. Wentworth represents other rock stars like Paul Stanley, the late Ric Ocasek of the Cars, and Mickey Hart from the Grateful Dead. They even rep the renowned artists Peter Max, Michael Godard, and Romero Britto. I am honored to be in all their company.

I started something else that has become very important to me. As I've written here, there have been times when I attempted to manage young, up-and-coming bands and produce the records. It never really came together the way I wanted it to, but in 2017 that all changed. I decided it was time to really take the idea seriously of creating an entertainment/management label that would let me act as a one-stop shop for young bands. I would develop young bands, write songs with them, produce them in my studio, engineer, and even manage them. Hell, I had been managing Tesla at that point for ten years, so I knew what the hell needed to be done. Starting my own label just seemed like a natural progression. I had learned from so many guys over the years, except none of those guys were really musicians (except for Terry Thomas). To me, a producer especially is much better at the job when they are a musician, because they speak our language. They can really get something out of musicians because they know what they're talking about. I got Jimmy Dean to help me launch J Street Music Group because he's so smart and hard-working. Away we went. So far it's been a really great experience for both of us. It's a lot of work, but it's something I think I can really expand in the future. I think I provide a service that is so top-to-bottom, and I have so much experience in all these areas that I'm qualified take a band and help shape their future at every level. I like hard work, so I love all the shit. I'm all about the ability to diversify. I may not be able to play bass in a band for the rest my life. But I'm always going to want to be creative. So whether I'm painting, taking photographs, or helping guide the way for the next hot band, I will never be stagnant creatively.

Balancing Act

The health issues I have to deal with are primarily from stress. It's a taxing thing to be the guy who has to keep shit together. They don't know what causes my autoimmune disorder. The condition I have is ulcerated colitis, which means your immune system attacks itself, and it manifests itself in the intestines and the joints. My ankles swell up, all kinds of weird shit. Colitis attacks just your intestines; Crohn's Disease, which I also was recently diagnosed with on top of everything else, is from your esophagus to colon, that's the only difference. It's all inflammation. Anxiety and stress are the main triggers. Today I feel things are pretty stable, and my stress levels are down.

By 2018 we needed a break because we had been going at it hard for the last four or five years, but then we were going to take six months off. The new record was recorded and was being mixed, and we'd been banging the shit out while touring the last three years with Def Leppard. Phil Collen said, "Let's get the fuck out there and make some hay." That was his whole thing; he became our guru. There's not a lot of bands left like us; let's go out there and get all the fans. Instead of run down and fuck one, let's walk down and fuck 'em all, so that's what we're doing.

Old Dogs, New Tricks

We hit the road again with Leppard and REO Speedwagon. We continued the same demo process that we used for "Save That Goodness." Phil had a big part in that because as an opening act on a three-band production, we only had two dressing rooms. Phil made sure we got a third room to use as a recording studio at most of the shows, a room that Leppard would have had. Our British brothers were pitching in to help us out.

We'd go in there before sound checks, which usually hit at around four in the afternoon. So if we got to the venue at two, that gave us a couple of hours to get some work done. It could be anyone's idea on any given day: mine, Phil's, Frank's, Dave's. Phil would collaborate with Jeff on some lyrics for guide vocals, and then I'd lay down a drum program using an app called Slate.

When we came off the road, we had everything sketched out, and we recorded proper masters at J Street. It was a two-year process, which was different than anything we'd done before. Previously it was more about getting the whole time as compacted as possible, maybe four or five months from start to finish. This new album would be a lot more organic and relaxed. And because it was recorded while we were playing every night on stage, it brought a live energy as well.

Being together on the bus and at the gigs had an effect too. Where before, a song would be mostly one guy's composition and structure, the new album featured a lot more collaboration from that road environment, and that includes Phil too. Every single song on the album had Phil as co-writer. Phil brought a lot of knowledge and experience that he'd absorbed from the Leppard albums produced by Mutt Lange. Because he's an intelligent guy, Phil customized those things for Tesla, not just recreated them. He had a great relationship with Jeff, which may be the most critical piece of the Tesla puzzle. He would tell us that he was always impressed with the ability we had to play our instruments. And not just in a safe, conservative style, but that we were up to try anything. Both the band and Phil really enjoyed that, because we were both stepping outside of our formulas and habits. It was a lot of ideas and workflows that were coming to us from all angles. It both allowed and forced us to be open to new concepts and ways of working. The whole process was so different that Phil and I wrote a song about it called "Comfort Zone."

The extra time allowed the band members to help with lyric writing, which was great for Jeff because it relieved a major source of pressure on him. That's a responsibility he has had since day one, and the stress of it takes a toll. And as you've read here, it caused problems from time to time, both for the band and for him emotionally.

Jeff will always be the most identifiable element of Tesla's sound. Many bands have this same identity focus. Think Steven Tyler or Joe Elliott. Even though the band internally might be a democracy, the public perception comes from the voice. You know right away who you're listening to, even if it's an acoustic version or a re-arrangement. There's one track on *Shock* called "California

Summer Song" that sounds like it could have been written by Sublime, but the instant Jeff starts singing, you know it's Tesla.

I think *Shock* strikes a good balance between the traditional Tesla sound and the contemporary environment that is important to remain vital in today's market. Phil understood that balance out of the gate. He's been in our world since 1987, on our third tour supporting our first album. He's a peer, of our generation, grew up listening to much of the same music as we did, and so having many of the same influences and musical heroes.

Even though *Shock* was complete, the release date wasn't until the fall of 2018. We had a summer tour with Styx and Joan Jett, but we didn't do any material from the new album. We don't really like to introduce new material live that people can't buy or hear on the radio, because what's the point?

Tables Turned

We have not discussed this, but I'm scared shitless of flying. When I was six years old I witnessed a horrible plane crash. It got a lot of national news coverage. It occurred at an air show that was happening at the Sacramento Executive Airport in South Sacramento. An F-86 Sabre fighter jet lost power on takeoff and skidded into an ice cream parlor that was across the street directly in line with the runway. Twenty-three people, including twelve children at a birthday party, were killed and dozens more injured. I saw the explosion and the towering flames from the jet fuel, heard screaming and people dying. Since that day I have been terrified of flying.

We were heading to Texas in 2006 to make *Real to Reel*, and I was fairly well medicated to get through the flight from Sacramento to El Paso. When I got to the studio, all the usual suspects were there: Frank, Troy was putting his drum kit together, Tom Zutaut was puttering around, Michael Rosen was waiting to mic things up. I was still a little out of it from the flight when I noticed this skinny little English kid. Michael said, "Brian, I want you to meet Jimmy Dean. He's here from England doing an internship."

I said, "Hi, Jimmy Dean."

He said, "Hello, mate." Needing a pick-me-up, I asked Jimmy Dean if he'd make me a cup of tea. He said sure, do I want cream and sugar? I did, so he went away and got me the tea.

The next day I walked in the studio, and he's got a cup of tea already made for me, with just the right amount of cream and sugar. That was enough for me to take a liking to him. During the session Frank walks over to me and says, "I really like this Jimmy Dean kid." He was a young gentleman and was ambitious with a respectful manner. He was perceptive too. He saw things that were needed and took care of them. And he was a people person. He was about twenty-two at the time and kind of crazy, doing more than his share of drugs and partying. He had long, dark, straight hair like Bob Seger.

When I'd go into El Paso on an errand, Jimmy Dean would come along. He told me about growing up in England. He was in an odd little band for a while. They'd take drums and flutes and stuff into these caves and chant and bang the drums. He also told me his real name was Dean Robson. Rosen came up with Jimmy Dean. We talked about my studio in Sacramento, and one day he asked if he could intern there. I called Monique and told her about the kid and his desire to intern at the studio, which hadn't burned down yet. He'd have to live in our house since I wasn't going to be paying him anything. Because Monique is such an awesome person and wife, she said if I thought it was a good idea then she was all for it.

He came out to Sacramento and was there when we recorded Volume 2 of *Real to Reel*. I took a real liking to the kid, and he was super helpful. After a few months his work visa ran out, and he had to go back to England. We were preparing to go out on tour, and Tom wanted to record all the shows. I proposed that we bring Jimmy Dean with us and let him handle the recording. So back over to the States he came.

It was during this time that we fired Tom Zutaut. We were booked to do shows in England, but Tom never set any of the logistics up: no visas, no flights, no hotels, no transport, no merchandising, nothing. So I called up Jimmy Dean, who'd gone back to England after the tour ended. I said, "Jimmy Dean, can you help us out?"

And he said, "No worries mate, I'll get right on it." And he did. He probably had no idea how to do a lot of what he had to do, but that didn't stop him. What he didn't know, he figured out and got it done.

After we were done with the England shows, Steve Emler, our sound engineer who was doubling as road manager, told me we should hire the kid to road manage. Obviously Steve thought he was a good fit and could handle it. He said he could tutor Jimmy Dean and turn him into a great road manager.

When Tesla got signed to Geffen and started touring, we always had experienced road managers whose job it was to keep the lunatics under control, meaning the band! Over all the years in the '80s and '90s we had all kinds of different road managers, some really good and some not so much. But they all had a kind of authority status, and the band would mostly just do whatever they wanted without question. After all those years, we realized we didn't need or want that kind of relationship with our road manager. We wanted somebody who was more concerned with what *we* wanted, and could get that done properly, as well as represent and fight for us when those kinds of situations arose. After several misfires after we reformed in 2000, I believed we might have found the right guy in Jimmy Dean.

He went through the process of getting his green card, and Steve started mentoring him while we were on the road. We made him the road manager in 2006. Because we had our own record label, Tesla Electrical Company Recording, or TECR, I started educating Jimmy on that side of the business. We'd sit in the production office on the road and work on radio promotion and in-store appearances and all that stuff. He got a real crash course in the modern music industry. It's been over sixteen years now, and he's kicking ass. He stopped doing drugs and bought a house in Sacramento. He even cut his long hair off. He's like my son now. Today he could tour manage almost anybody, he's gotten that good.

Working with Jimmy gave me a new perspective on my career path and where I was in my life. Being in a successful rock band can bring out selfish tendencies and habits, but I realized I was getting a deep satisfaction out of imparting all this knowledge and experience that I had absorbed over the years, and as a result, helping somebody turn from a young kid into a man and a professional. I imagine that is how Steve Clausman must have felt when he was managing City Kidd. Payback. Or as they say these days, paying it forward.

I met another kid who came out with a band from Iowa to record at J Street. Brett Stezil was a roadie for the band, and they treated him like shit, ordering him around, being disrespectful, even mean. On top of that, they sucked. They were so bad that after one day of recording, I told them that I was going to give them their money back and send them home. They were that awful. The drummer was the typical I-can't-play-worth-a-shit-so-I-have-a-lot-of-drums dude.

The night the band arrived at the studio, I took them out for pizza. Brett was sitting next to me, and I noticed a lip tattoo on his neck. I asked him, "What the fuck is with the lips on your neck?" He said they were his ex-wife's lips. I told him, "That's the dumbest thing I've ever seen. From now on, I'm fucking calling you Lipps."

While I was attempting to get something decent out of them in the studio, I asked Lipps if he'd go down to the garage and straighten it out. Over the years it had become a real mess, with shit all over the place, disorganized and dirty. About three hours later I went out there, and the fuckin' garage looked like Costco! Everything was cleaned up, on shelves, and organized into categories and sections.

He told me that he didn't want to go back to Iowa, and could I help him stay in California? I thought about it and told him, sure, he could live with me and Monique, and I would pay him to paint the house, which had a real intricate nine-color design. I asked him if he could do that paint job. He said, "Sure, I can do anything you want." Now that's an attitude I love, *but*, if you say it, you'd better be able to back it up, because I'm going to hold you to it, and I'm going to push you to go even further. You may not think you can, but if I do, chances are you will. That's a Clausie thing too.

It had been years since Jimmy Dean moved out of the house, and quite frankly, Monique and I missed having young energy around. Having Lipps move in seemed like a fairly natural thing to do. He's worked out so well that he moved to Baird with me and Monique. He's helped build and paint the new barn and paint the house. He and Jimmy are really like my two sons.

Jack, the guy I hired to run the studio in Sacramento, is a young dude as well. I'm definitely giving him a once-in-a-lifetime opportunity to do it any way he wants, and he's earned my trust in that. He makes good decisions, has an even temperament, and he's growing the business. He came to me with a high-functioning skill set already, and I'm always there to talk about things when he wants, but he's independent, and it's a great peace of mind to not have to worry about the studio.

A big thing with me and these guys is, if I ask you to do something a specific way, then do it that way. Don't go off track because you think you've got a better idea. Let me be the one who fucks up, not you, because whatever you're working on, it belongs to me or it's got my name on it. In other words, the buck always stops with me. All three guys understand that and are OK with it.

Maybe Jimmy Dean has earned his spurs to tell me he thinks I'm wrong. That's part of his growth, and I'm proud to see it in him, but that doesn't mean he and I don't have the occasional shouting match.

There's one more guy who's come into our lives recently: Jonathan. Lipps met him here in Sacramento and introduced me to him. He's a real muscular, quiet dude from Hawaii. Turned out he is a hell of a handyman and construction guy. At the time, we were getting ready to move to Texas, and I wanted to turn some of the rooms of our house in Sacramento into 'bnb rentals. I needed walls put up, plumbing and electrical put in, and Jonathan slid right in and did it. He lives at the house there and runs the property for me.

When we made the move to Texas, Jonathan drove one of the small fleet of trucks I had rented. He was at the new house unpacking one day when the doorbell rang. It was a reporter from the Abilene newspaper wanting to do a story about the rock star moving to Baird. Jonathan just kind of gave him this cold stare as he tried to get past the front door. He told the guy, "Mister Wheat has moved here to have privacy and does not want to be disturbed. If you give me your business card, I will see that he gets it." With that, he shut the door. I think Jonathan enjoyed doing that. I know I enjoyed watching him.

Epilogue

It's been said that life can be like a merry-go-round: enjoyable, safe, predictable. Or it can be like a roller coaster: up and down, fast and slow, whipping through turns that make your eyes water. My life certainly has not been a merry-go-round.

Some cultures look at life as being divided into thirds. For me the first third was developing a passion for music and becoming a professional musician. The second third was maturing in a way that allowed me to take ownership of my career and life. And the third third? Well, that's what is ahead of me in a few years and what I'm preparing for now. Almost certainly it will involve the end of constant touring and living in a tour bus. Does that mean the end of Tesla? Of course not. The band can easily go on without me on stage. But all the rest of the necessary tasks? I don't know if they could deal with what I do. Jimmy Dean could handle some of it. Phil Collen can run recording sessions; he's proven that. But the hard-core negotiations, the business relationships, the truth-telling? If Mike Kobayashi was not involved, someone would have to step up. I really don't know.

Soulmotor will live on as a partnership between Darin and me. We have a good thing going that I can easily control, and we can play live or not, as much or as little as we want.

I'm lucky in that I have gotten to see the world. I've been pretty much around the planet, but there are some places I haven't been that I'd like to go. Never went to or played in Russia; I'd like to go there, St. Petersburg, see the Hermitage museum, see all the art, all the palaces. That will probably happen, but I don't know if Tesla will get the chance to go. I think I'll go on my own. I went on my own to a lot of places that Tesla hasn't played: Bangkok, Vietnam, Burma. I haven't been to Singapore, but I've been to Hong Kong. I need to go to Shanghai. I've been to Dubai. Tesla played Australia, but I didn't get to hang out much. It didn't really feel like a foreign country to me. It kind of reminded me of Los Angeles. Melbourne had more of a European feel to it. I hear Christchurch in New Zealand has an English feel.

I like to go places where you feel like you're in a different country. Burma was that way; it was a trippy place to be. I was in the capital city, Rangoon, and shot some really cool pictures of temples with Ross. In Vietnam I went to Ho Chi Minh City, which used to be Saigon. That was very interesting, very cool. I went to Havana before it was legal. I snuck in. That was fucking cool, lots of old cars. I want to go to Morocco and Kashmir. I have no desire really to go to the rest of India or the Middle East. It just doesn't speak to me, but I'd like to go to parts of Africa. I really want to go to Russia. You can do the Chernobyl tour if you go to Ukraine, but I don't want to get nuked.

I'll never retire. As Douglas MacArthur said about old soldiers, I'll just fade away. I love old George Patton, but I hope I don't go out like he did, in a car accident. I have a compulsion to stay busy and vital. At the same time, I dearly love being able to just fly off to Tuscany and shut down. In the future I'll have more freedom to do that whenever I want. Or just tool around the peaceful Baird compound.

When I say *I*, I really mean *we* because my wife is my life partner and my best friend. Living in the shadow of my career has not always been easy for her. And I'm not that easy to handle, even if I had never achieved the success I have. I might have been the most temperamental accountant you ever met! So that's the deal. What else can I tell you? That's my life. I'm really proud of my band. I'm really happy I met my wife, and I love what our dogs bring to us in terms of loyalty and unconditional love. And I will always work my ass off no matter what. That's what has always defined my band and me. We work our asses off. We are blue-collar. That's the defining quality of Tesla, a work ethic that never stops. If you can bring the kick-ass work ethic, I will give you a chance. Look, life can be hard. In my situation, I deal with a lot of ailments and things that could really slow me down or worse. There have been times when I thought about ending it all, but I fight back because I believe in myself, and I believe in working hard. There's always something else to do. Whether it's music, photography or painting.... There's always something to do. Maybe it's a new house I'm looking at. As long as I feel like I have things to keep me busy, I will have a good life. If you suffer from any kind of mental disorder like depression, bipolar, general anxiety, anything, there is no shame in that. It's just another something to deal with, and it *can* be dealt with. Don't let anybody tell you otherwise. You can get past it. Find yourself a good therapist. Figure out who your good friends and family are. Don't be afraid to lean on them. The social media age we live in makes it very hard to cope with a lot of this shit. I've seen myself get attacked by fans goofing on the fact that I look overweight, which oftentimes is because of medications I'm taking for one thing or another. I would love to tell you it doesn't matter, but you know what? It's fucking brutal. We are all human beings, and we all have feelings. Social media makes it so easy to demean somebody and shame them in ways that were never possible before. There are so many cruel people out there who hide behind their computer and just love taking shots at people. If you have an anxiety disorder like I have, it makes it that much worse. Listen to me, especially those of you going through things like I am: you are stronger than they are. Don't let them get you. Walk away from the computer and go focus on a project that will make your life better. Don't ever let a bully get to you. They're just fucking cowards. When I stand on stage and look out at the crowd, which I'm sure includes many of you reading right now, I think, *Wow, I'm just one of them. I am just the lucky guy who gets to be up here.* If I can leave you with anything right now, I just want you to believe in yourself. I want you to take advantage of any resource that you can to help yourself feel better. Once again, I'm a great believer in the power of therapy. It hurts my heart to read the news every day and see how suicides are on the rise when I know one of the primary reasons is bullying. You just have to hang in there. I am living proof that you can get through all kinds of bullshit and realize dreams that border on fantasy. You can do this. I promise you can do this. We're all joined in this crazy mess together. I wish all of you the peace and strength you need to get through another day. And thanks very much for reading my book.

Ciao!

PS: At the beginning of this book, I described the scene with Chris Cornell, driving around with him during the photo shoot and then how strange it was to learn he committed suicide. After the first draft of this book was completed, while we were on the road with Def Leppard, I felt the depression creep up in Canada. It was unlike anything I'd ever felt before. I knew it was getting bad because of how much I wanted to sleep. That's all I wanted to do was stay in that coffin of a bunk on the tour bus. I never wanted to get up. Like a dark claw, the feeling just kept creeping over me every day. I didn't know what was happening, but I knew it wasn't good, and I knew it was something more intense than anything I'd felt before. I've experienced general anxiety many times in my life, but I'd never really felt suicidal. But up in Canada, all of a sudden, the idea was at least on the table. I'm not saying I was ready to end my life, but again, I could see the idea developing right in front of me, and I didn't like it one bit. I got help. I spoke to a professional. There are too many stories today about people taking the hard way out and ending things. If you are reading this right now, I want to stress once more that you're not alone. There is help, and you can get it immediately. I know talking logic and sense doesn't always make sense because for those of us who experience these feelings, it's all very illogical. We know it's not good to think about killing ourselves. But it doesn't matter. The feeling is there anyway. Someone making a positive reinforcement speech to you is not always what you need to hear. Sometimes we just need someone to listen to us. And then we can start sorting the problems. I think back to that tour up in Canada all the time, and it's still really scary. Again, that was the first time I ever really thought about maybe creating an end for myself. But I got the right help, and I'm feeling a lot better today. I'm going to include some numbers here at the end of my book that you can use in case you need help. Please remember, you are not alone.

National Suicide Prevention Lifeline: 1-800-273-8255
The Crisis Text Line can be reached by texting HOME *to* 741-741

AFTERWORD

BY ROSS HALFIN

I first met Brian Wheat in 1986. I was in NYC, and Peter Mensch (Manager to the Stars) told me he'd just signed a new band from Sacramento and asked me to shoot them. His words were, "They need some direction, and hide the bass player at the back." So I met up with what looked like a group that had styled themselves at Walmart. They had no clue and were just annoyingly naive and completely uncultured. We walked around, and as I do, I'm trying to get some form of connection, and there was *none*. The only one who seemed to have any idea of what I was trying to do was the bass player; the others just followed me moronically. At one point I lined them in the back of a meat truck, and as they were lined up a black woman appeared in a robe. She opened it to reveal that she was naked, grabbed one of her breasts, and said something like "I've just had a baby, any of you want any milk?" She squeezed her breast, and a stream of milk shot out. She then offered to blow all of us for ten dollars each. Me being me, I was like, "Why don't you fuck off?" The band looked genuinely excited at the prospect, far more than being photographed by me, but none of them had any money, and

I was asked if I could come up with twenty dollars. Taking charge, I'm like, *no*. I called Mensch up afterwards and said, "I never want to see this band again."

Of course, they ended up being the openers on the Def Leppard *Hysteria* tour, and I still didn't like any of them apart from the bass player, Brian, who I started hanging out with on most of the tour. In fact, if I went out it was always with Steve Clark and then Brian would come along. I ended up shooting Tesla in England when they first came over. I did sessions for them on the West Coast, and in Los Angeles, even a weekend in Sacramento where Tommy Skeoch decided he was Keith Richards, which meant he took as many pills as possible and turned up the whole weekend falling down drugged and drunk. On the last day I saw him at the bar, I took him aside and said, "Why are you doing this?"

He looked at me and said, "I am Rock 'n' Roll."

My actual reply was, "Rock 'n' Roll? You're just a stupid cunt."

Jeff Keith had arrived by then and was like, "Hey, don't pick on my brother Tommy."

I said "Enough, I'm done," and I've never seen him since. Brian, who by now had had enough, looked at me and I went berserk.

He said "Honestly, I'm trying." I ended up not shooting Tesla again for years, but we always stayed friendly, although from afar.

I went through a really bad personal period in 2006, and out of the blue Brian called me, whom I totally did not want to talk to, but he could tell that I was not in a good space. Much to my surprise he got on a plane and came to England and stayed with me as a friend. Let me point out that in my business, I can count my real friends on one hand. Since then we've become very close. I've spent a few Christmases with him in Sacramento and London, and we got into the habit, which I'm rather pleased with, of picking somewhere in the world and going off to it, places like Vietnam, Thailand, Burma, Japan. The only thing wrong with traveling with him is I like to get up at dawn, and he thinks the day starts at 3:00 p.m. My other great passion in later life is collecting vinyl, as does Brian, which we both seem to have regressed to our youth, listening to bands we grew up on. Although he's still trying to make me like the Beatles, a band I loathe.

Let me just finish with this: in anyone's life there are very few real friends, and Brian is truly a real friend of mine, someone who I can always count on.

POST SCRIPT

A lot has happened since I finished writing this book. For one thing, I moved from Texas to upstate New York. Not only that, I made the move during the coronavirus quarantine. So let's just say as I'm sitting here right this minute it's been pretty crazy. But we are getting settled, and all is well. We still got the place in Texas and will be back once in a while, but by now you know how I am with big old houses, and I found one in New York that I just could not resist. I'll admit my health issues are getting severely challenged by this current crisis. Shit, we lost a huge Alice Cooper tour as well as lots of headlining—and not just my band; the crew, the people who work at the venues, the merch people, everybody. As I'm sure all of you know, this thing is hitting everybody hard. But you know what? We're a strong fucking country and will be back soon. I've had a lot of moments to think in the last couple of months with all of this free time, and that's helped me focus on who I would like to thank for being in my life and making the story even possible. Listen, if I have forgotten you on this list, please don't take it personally. You know how I am. I'm just doing my best. I'll make it up to you next time I see you. But in the meantime, my life would not have been the same without the following people....

ACKNOWLEDGMENTS

I have many people to acknowledge, but listen, if for some reason I've forgotten to add your name here, don't take it personally. Let me know when I see you and I'll buy you a beer. Got it?

Here we go: To my mother, Amelia, for always loving me; Monique, for standing behind me through thick and thin; Sandi, I'm so happy we're friends again; my dad for letting me out of his pants (ha ha); and also to Buddy, Sheri, Mike, David, Timmy, Gary, Butch, Cecil Cayocca, Paulette, Ethel Hoy, Kay Fessenden, Shirley Jackson, Dr. Scott, Mike Johnson DVM, John, Victor and Terry, Frank Jeff, Troy, Dave, Mike Kobayashi, Chris Epting, Jacob Hoye and the team at Post Hill Press, Ken "Gus" Nicholson, Brett "Lipps" Stetzel, Jack O'Donnell, Terry Munoz, Mike Verras, Chris Johns, Colleen and Sally, Marvin Morris, Tommy Whitecotten, the Porro family, the Kelly family, Nicola, Paulo, Mike Brown, Dave Stieh, Def Leppard, Joe Elliott, Phil Collen, Ross Halfin, Oliver Halfin, Kazio, Peter Makowski, Jimmy Page, Pete Way, Tom Zutaut, Teresa Ensanat, Steve Thompson, Michael Barbiero, Terry Thomas, Michael Rosen, Rick Jackson, Dave Dittman, Steve Clausman, Brian Clausman, Mike Clausman, Dan McClendon, Tommy McClendon, Pat Travers, Peter Torza, Julene Silva, Darin Wood, Derik Deisen, Jolene Martin, Christian O'Mahoney, Victor Somogyi, Tony D, Adam Kornfeld, Steve Strange, Joni Soekotjo, Joe Peterson, Cliff Burnstein, Peter Mensch, Steve Emler, Marko Bustos, Larry Shure, Krank Lawson, Taz, Pat & Monica Martin, Thea & Dixon, Keith & Pat Sims, Bonnie & Clyde, Spanky & Darla, Thelma & Louise, Alfalfa, Mrs. Bollinger, Alex, TC, Jim Cuomo, Dr. Faddoul, Isaac Herschkopp, Ed Flores, Mark Johannesen, Hofner basses, D'Addario strings, and, last but not least, the Beatles, Led Zeppelin, and Queen for inspiring me.

ABOUT THE AUTHORS

Brian Wheat is best known as the bass guitarist of the platinum-selling band, Tesla, which he co-founded in 1982. Tesla became one of the biggest bands of the late 1980s–1990s. Brian owns a recording studio by the name of J Street Recorders in Sacramento, California. Papa Roach, Tesla, Pat Travers, Deftones, Kodiak Jack, Flashfires, and many others have recorded there.

Chris Epting is an award-winning journalist and the author of many books, including *Adrenalized* (co-written with Def Leppard's Phil Collen) and *Change of Seasons* (co-written with John Oates).